A GUIDEBOOK FOR ADVANCED ANGEL READINGS

Elizabeth J. Foley

D1502102

Transform yourself from
merely an experienced reader
into a Divine Oracle

Published and distributed in the United States by Angel Street Publishing, LLC, P.O. Box 7298, Nashua, NH 03060 ♥ www.angelstreetpublishing.net.

Material excerpted from the book *Dear God What Is Happening To Us?* *By Lynn Grabhorn* ©2003, with permission of Hampton Roads Publishing Company, Inc., c/o Red Wheel/Weiser, LLC, Newburyport, MA and San Francisco, CA, www.redwheelweiser.com, #800-423-7087.

Book design by Robin Wrighton ♥ www.robinwrighton.com
Printed by: King Printing Company, Inc. ♥ www.kingprinting.com

Front cover image: An Angel Playing a Flageolet, 1878 (w/c, gouache and gold on paper) by Sir Edward Burne-Jones (1833-98)
©Sudley House, National Museums Liverpool/The Bridgeman Art Library

Back cover image provided by Lee Lewalski

A Guidebook for Advanced Angel Readings / Elizabeth J. Foley

ISBN 10: 0-9800806-4-9
ISBN 13: 978-0-9800806-4-3

April 2010

Printed in the United States of America

Contents

FOREWORD

If you are picking up this book at this point in time, it is probably because a series of synchronistic events led you here. You may have picked up a package of angel oracle cards and found the results fascinating, and now you want to take your knowledge to the next level. Nothing happens by accident. When you work with the angelic realm you quickly learn that everything happens in Divine order.

I met Elizabeth Foley through a series of synchronistic events. I had called my local Barnes and Nobles bookstore to see if they had a copy of *Ask Your Guides* by Sonia Chocquette to give to a friend going through a tough job search. I tried and tried to get through by phone and finally I said to myself, "Too upstream. You must want me to be there in person for some reason," speaking to my own angel team. I had just started working with angels as a result of reading Sonia Chocquette's book and listening to Doreen Virtue on Hay House Radio.

I jumped in my car and went to my local Barnes and Noble book store. I found the last copy of the book *Ask Your Guides* on the shelf and proceeded to the check out area when a sign caught my attention, "Author of *Angel Readings for Beginners* and *Awakening the Lightworker Within* Here Today." I said to myself, "Hmmm...now I know why I had to come in." Sure enough, Elizabeth was just about to kick off her book signing presentation. "How timely," I smiled knowing there were no accidents. I popped my head into her group to see if there was a seat available and noticed the room was packed. Elizabeth saw me peek in and said, "Come on in. As a matter of fact, there is one more open chair right here in front of me."

When the student is ready, the teacher will appear...and have a seat waiting for you right up front! From that day on, I got to know Elizabeth, take her classes and become an Advanced Angel Healing Practitioner through the certification program she teaches. Life has never been the same since. All because I paid attention to the signs from the angels.

The angels are now giving you a sign that they want you to advance in your spiritual development and your knowledge of them. Know that this book is your ticket to advanced guidance and wisdom that can only come from a close connection to a wise teacher and mentor.

You picked up *A Guidebook for Advanced Angel Readings* and have read thus far, so know that this book was written just for you. It's time for you to explore your connection with the angelic realm in more depth with the intention that the student will eventually become the teacher and healer.

Elizabeth Foley, the Master Teacher, will only show up in your life when you are ready and class begins now.

Robin Rousseau
Explore Beyond the Usual™

INTRODUCTION

D o you feel ready to take your angel readings to a more advanced level? If so, this book was written just for you, as an opportunity to learn and explore techniques that will help deepen your spiritual connection and take your readings to a higher and more expansive level.

In these pages, you will find information about the celestial hierarchy, and explore advanced reading techniques such as channeling, mediumship and Akashic Records just to name a few. You will also find details on advanced self-care techniques, tips to assist you in building your angel reading practice, and the code of ethics for conducting both free and paid readings.

As you know, it takes strong foundations to support successful growth and consistent practice of the techniques revealed in my earlier book, *Angel Readings for Beginners*, will have given you precisely that. If you haven't already read it, take the time to do so. You'll find it a wonderful resource tool with clear instructions for laying in that excellent groundwork, even for experienced readers!

Over time, you have probably crafted a reading style that is uniquely your own. This book can help you to refine your style, yet its true purpose is refinement of your intuition. Practicing these techniques with pure, positive intent spurs your own spiritual growth, and more profound readings are a natural result.

My own introduction to angel readings came by accident. One day I casually picked up a deck of angel oracle cards, and at the time I wasn't sure what the word "oracle" meant...so I thought that this new deck of cards was some type of a game. That's right–a game! I did not know that I held in the palm of my hand a very powerful tool to help me create a relationship and conversation with my own angels. Of course, I now smile as I recall my mistake because in truth, there are no mistakes.

Once I realized what these cards were and what I could do with them, each day I talked with my angels to get messages for myself. Angel cards truly changed my life because they initiated the habit of communing with the angels.

All these years later, even though my intuitive abilities have grown stronger, I still like working with cards when doing readings, even for myself. I find that when used during a session, the cards provide visual validation. They also help clients to connect with, understand and remember the reading as well as the messages.

For example, during one session, Archangel Michael communicated to me that my client was a Lightworker and requested that I introduce her to him.

Although of course I dutifully delivered the messages from Michael, this young lady had a look of puzzlement on her face. She did understand my words–the problem was that she'd never heard of Archangel Michael! Without any frame of reference, it was very difficult for her to process or connect with the message. So, Michael instructed me that it was time to work with the oracle cards. The very moment I began, the Archangel Michael card literally flew out of the deck. Ahh! Now my client had a visual! The images opened a world of understanding for my client, as the cards have done for me and so many others.

I'm sharing this story to remind you that your cards remain unique and effective tools for readings, even as we explore other ways and means of tapping into your intuitive gifts.

Now there is an essential point that must be clearly understood. Once you decide to do a reading for someone, the angels and other Beings of Light take your intention and action very seriously, for you are that Divine Messenger for them. They will do anything to assist you with your reading. Just as you prepare yourself for your angel session, your angelic team is also preparing to work with you. Always invite the angels in and allow them to fully participate in your sessions. Let the angelic magic unfold, for with each reading you will discover, as I did, there is always something new to learn from your angelic partners.

Remember, they too want success for you and will support you throughout the whole process. The angels say, "Failure is not an option when you work with us." They will work with your energy and whatever reading tools you choose to use. The Illuminated Ones are doing their part, you now need to do yours, which is what the book you now hold in your hands can help you with.

As mentioned before, you will find your own reading style changing and shifting along your spiritual path and evolution.

Indeed, as you practice more and speak with the angels daily, you will discover and rediscover some of your own hidden talents, perhaps it could be the gift of being a teacher or healer in your readings. Anything and everything is possible. Just be open!

It is my sincere hope that the information contained in these pages will help to guide you along your journey to being that Divine Messenger and Spiritual Ambassador for God and the Earth.

DEEPENING YOUR SPIRITUAL CONNECTION

Now that you have been working with your angels for a while, it is time to deepen your spiritual connection with these Beings of Light. Remember, your angelic team is not limited to angels and archangels. You can invite God, the Divine Source of All, Ascended Masters such as Sananda or Kuthumi, spirit guides, power animals, and other non-physical Beings of Light to participate in your work.

In truth, they are present all the time. It is we who often dull our awareness of the Divine with fear, ego and our inordinate focus on life's dramas. However, when we choose to place our attention on our heavenly helpers, the veil between the worlds becomes thinner, even vanishing altogether in exceptional moments. The adventure of life certainly continues, yet we navigate its twists and turns with growing ease, humility and joy.

Currently, we are all in a critical time of ascension and spiritual evolution. This means we are in the process of moving from a third dimension of human consciousness to a higher dimension. It is therefore essential to refine our bodies of Light, which intensifies our own spiritual connection to the Divine and our Higher Self or God Self.

Daily meditation on the Light robustly links us to the source of our being. When we permit our consciousness to merge with the Higher Self, the result is greater access to the priceless information contained within. Divine Intelligence always guides us and answers our deepest questions.

We become a strong and coherent energy field of Light, which is conveyed in our interactions with others as a constant state of peace and harmony in an unspoken way.

When you are Light's purest intention, there is no confusion, no mistake.

Here are some specific methods that can assist you with raising your vibration, shifting your consciousness to higher levels and deepening your own personal connection.

1. Invite and connect with your angels on a daily basis. This is done by setting your intention and inviting them in to work with you.

2. Make prayer and meditation a daily practice.

3. Remember to stay in the Light as often as you can. See yourself as being Light and call the Light into yourself.

4. Practice compassionate detachment from personal and worldly drama.

5. Keep shedding away the internal layers of mental and emotional toxins through working with your angelic team and with the transformational tools that you have studied.

6. Learn to attune to your higher guidance by stilling mental chatter.

7. Clear, clean, align and balance your chakras and para-chakras daily.

8. Ask your spiritual team of angels, guides and Ascended Masters to work with you in the ethers while you sleep. You can ask permission to journey to the appropriate inner temples or ashrams of the Masters for your own learning.

When you sincerely invite the Divine more fully into your life, let your heart stay open to recognizing its presence in both subtle and surprising ways. You may begin to notice synchronicities or coincidences more often, or you may feel wings brush against your face or hands, see brilliant flashes of light, or unexpectedly smell a beautiful fragrance wafting in the air. Perhaps you may even sense the room or space suddenly seeming lighter, bringing you the experience of inner peace and Divine bliss.

Over time, daily communication with your spiritual team will enhance your overall wellbeing, increase your Light quotient, deepen and accelerate your spiritual growth, evolution and ascension process–and positively impact your readings!

STRENGTHENING YOUR INTUITIVE POWER

D o you remember the test I challenged you with in the *Angel Readings for Beginners* book? Is there a difference between someone who is psychic and someone who is intuitive? Now take a moment to think about this before you continue. When you think you know the answer, then you may continue to read.

The word "psyche" comes from the Greek language and it means "soul." Everyone is psychic or has psychic potential. There is but one exception to this truth: When someone believes that they need to be a "special" person or possess "special powers," they will automatically block themselves from tapping into their own gifts.

Someone who is psychic can perceive information and energy around someone and read the energy; they will simply convey what they observe. An intuitive reader assesses the core beingness of the person they are reading for and then does a check in with their spiritual team asking, "Is this something I need to share or just to know?" The intuitive assesses the mental and emotional energy of the person and then asks, "Can this person handle what I am getting?" The bottom line is that an intuitive knows when to speak and when to stay silent. Just because you receive information does not mean you always have to share it! So I hope you become more of an intuitive angel reader using Divine discernment.

As you develop and tap into your own intuition, you begin to pass through the different phases of intuition.

The first phase of intuition is the Receptive Phase:

- The five senses (sight, sound, taste, touch and smell)

- The feelings (sadness, anger, fear, anxiety and happiness, etc.)

- Psychic gifts (clairvoyance, clairaudience, clairsentience and claircognizance)

- Inner knowing

All of these are vital and synthesized by your intuition.

The second phase of intuition is the Dynamic Phase, which uses Compassion and Wisdom to know:

- When to speak and when to stay silent

- How to share the information with another

- When to act (be a participant) and when not to act (be an observer)

In addition, the more you know and understand energy, the more you will begin to understand your own psychic gifts. For more specific information on your psychic abilities, please review the Psychic Gifts chapter in my book, *Angel Readings for Beginners.*

Psychic energy is linked to your chakras and the word "chakra" comes from Sanskrit, which means "spinning wheels." So, in essence, chakras are spinning wheels or vortexes of energy. The chakras are centered within your body and your energy field. Their purpose is to feed life-force energy to the body and nourish all the cells and organs of the body.

There are eight major chakras: root, sacral, solar plexus, heart, throat, third eye, ear and crown.

There are also four major para-chakras. The word "para" means "beyond," indicating that these chakras are beyond the physical body.

The four major para-chakras are the omega, alpha, terra and angelic. Now let's review each one so that you have a full understanding of your major energy centers.

THE EIGHT MAJOR CHAKRAS

Crown Chakra

Location: Crown or top of head

Color: Violet or White (White reflects the presence of strong claircognizance)

Psychic Gift: Claircognizance (clear knowing)

Function: The crown chakra is the center of our spirituality, enlightenment, dynamic thought and energy. It is the center that allows us to grasp spiritual concepts and esoteric information and is affected by our thoughts and feelings relating to God, religion, spirituality and Divine guidance.

Third Eye Chakra

Location: Between the eyes and just above the bridge of your nose

Color: Indigo Blue or Dark Blue

Psychic Gift: Clairvoyance (clear seeing)

Function: This chakra is often called the Brow chakra and allows one to see things as they really are because there is no emotional attachment to what is going on. Through our physical eyes, we see people and process it through our emotions. This chakra acts as our spiritual eyes to see truth in things, situations and people, and is affected by thoughts and feelings relating to the future, the past, and beliefs about the spirit world.

Ear Chakra

Location: One to two inches above the ear (near the temple line)

Color: Magenta

Psychic Gift: Clairaudience (clear hearing)

Function: The ear chakra gives us the ability to hear the voice of God, angels, guides, Ascended Masters, deceased loved ones and your Higher Self.

Throat Chakra

Location: Area of the Adam's Apple

Color: Light Blue or Sky Blue

Psychic Gift: None

Function: The throat chakra is where we communicate our truth and integrity to the external world. This chakra is affected by thoughts and feelings associated with speaking your truth, communication projects, and asking for your needs to be met.

Heart Chakra

Location: Center of the chest, at the level of the heart

Color: Emerald Green or Pink (reflects unconditional love of self and others)

Psychic Gift: None

Function: The heart chakra is all about Love. It is concerned with our thoughts and feelings about relationships, love, and forgiveness. As one moves into the heart, they become more concerned with experiencing peace, both within and in the external world.

Solar Plexus Chakra

Location:	Stomach area
Color:	Golden Yellow
Psychic Gift:	Clairsentience (clear feeling)
Function:	This energy center is the central point of your physical body for all the nerves and it is our powerhouse. If ever you feel drained, most likely energy was taken or drained from this chakra area. This chakra is affected by thoughts and feelings about power and control.

Sacral Chakra

Location:	Three to four inches below the solar plexus
Color:	Orange
Psychic Gift:	None
Function:	This energy point is concerned with getting our physical desires met. Your thoughts and feelings about cravings for physical pleasure, addictions and your body in general affect the sacral chakra.

Root Chakra

Location:	Base of the spine
Color:	Red

Psychic Gift: None

Function: This chakra is concerned only with physical survival and having your physical needs met. There is no reflection, reasoning or deeper interaction occurring. The primary concern is survival for the body (food, shelter, money, etc.).

THE FOUR PARA-CHAKRAS

Angelic Chakra

Location: Between 18 and 24 inches out from the top of our head

Color: Gold

Psychic Gift: None

Function: The angelic chakra contains the programming of the soul for this lifetime as well as the history of the soul. It is through our connection and understanding of this chakra that we gain or affect our own healings, insights, learn our lessons, understand the soul contracts and begin to understand our life purpose.

Alpha Chakra or Soul Star Chakra

Location: Between 12 and 18 inches out from the top of the head.

Color: Ultra Violet (Blue and Violet)

Psychic Gift: None

Function: This chakra is the access to information about karma, lessons, our learning abilities, doorways to dimensions and times as well as the Akashic Records. When we access past life information it is through this chakra. Occasionally we can access this information in the dream state, when there is important information to be communicated to us.

Omega Chakra

Location: Midway between the root chakra and the knees

Color: Infrared (Red and Blue)

Psychic Gift: None

Function: This is an energy transference chakra. It takes in energy from the world and other people, plants and animals and operates like a step-down or step-up transformer. The omega transfers energy from outside the body to the inside, increasing or decreasing it as necessary to stimulate energy flow and release blocks.

Terra Chakra

Location: Midway between the knees and the feet

Color: Silver

Psychic Gift: None

Function: It is through the terra chakra that we ground and connect to the Mother Earth. The terra chakra anchors us to the physical world.

All chakras must be equally balanced. We must work not only on the spiritual or upper chakras, but all of them equally. You can balance your chakras in various ways. Energy work, pendulum work and calling on your angels all work well, but I especially like the way most of us did this in Atlantean times. In that lifetime, we were fully aware of the power of thought and simply commanded what we needed or wanted. Try commanding your chakras by saying, "All of my chakras and para-chakras open, cleanse, align and balance now." Yes, it is just that easy and simple. You see, energy always follows thought and intention. So when you hold that thought and intention of balancing your chakras combined with commanding them to cleanse, align and balance, your energy centers automatically align and balance. If you love and appreciate simplicity, then try it.

As we begin our spiritual path, we may encounter fears that prevent our intuitive flow. With awareness and understanding of our personal fears, we can increase our ability to listen to and trust our intuition. Some of the fears that block us from tapping into and trusting our intuition include:

♦ Fear of failure or making a mistake, which brings about feelings of humiliation.

➤ Fear of success and having greater expectations and responsibilities.

➤ Lack of trusting oneself (ego versus soul).

➤ Belief that the message is illogical.

➤ Past experience of, "The last time I followed my gut feeling, it was wrong."

➤ The intuitive message doesn't (seem to) fit into the present plan or situation.

➤ Fear of entering into unknown territory.

➤ My intuition may ask or guide me to change.

When you are aware of fears or anxieties coming to the surface, embrace your feelings, be honest with yourself and call on Archangel Michael to remove any fears, blocks, anxieties and obstacles that are preventing you from making a connection and tapping into your intuitive power. Then elicit the assistance of Archangel Ariel, for her specialty is helping Lightworkers to heal their negative self-talk and self-sabotaging behaviors. She can infuse you with newfound courage and strength to walk your path and follow your journey home.

As you exercise your psychic gifts through play, you will strengthen and reinforce them. An example of playing with your intuition is predicting who is calling on the phone before you answer it or look at the caller ID. The next time you are waiting at a red light, try to guess how many seconds it will be before the red light changes to green. Another exercise you can try is take a deck of regular playing cards and pull one card out face down and try to get a sense and feel of the color, the number or image on the card. Once you think you have it, then turn the card over for validation.

These are some simple and fun ways to begin to awaken your own psychic potential.

Now these are all ways in which you can build your psychic abilities and gifts...but what about intuition? Remember there is a substantial difference between being psychic and intuitive.

Here is a true story that demonstrates the power of intuition.

Donna (*not her real name*) considered herself just a regular person. She worked in a hardware store, stocking the shelves. One day while at work she saw a man walk though the store door and she heard in her head, even though his mouth did not move, "I did it, I did it, I did it."

He noticed her and walked up and asked if the store carried any large plastic containers. She got a very bad, uneasy feeling about his inquiry. Donna responded with directions as to where such containers could be found in the store. He was pleasant and said, "Thank you." Once he found the containers, he took the merchandise to the cash register which was near to the shelves Donna was working on. He looked at her and she could hear that voice repeating the same message in her head, "I did it, I did it, I did it." Still feeling uneasy, Donna dismissed the strange experience.

A few days later, the same man walked through the door. Again, Donna heard the same message and got a strong gut feeling that something was not right. Her sense of uneasiness increased. As before, the man approached Donna for directions. However, this time he inquired about bags of concrete mix. She assisted him and when he returned to cash out, she heard that message in her head yet again, "I did it, I did it, I did it."

As he paid for the concrete, he turned to Donna and just looked at her. His look seemed to pierce her soul and made her feel sick to her stomach.

On her way home, she thought about this man, the message in her head and the products that he had purchased. She felt guided to contact the police. Explaining that she was not a psychic, Donna shared the words she had heard in her mind, along with the details of this person's purchases. She admitted that while she did not know what the message meant, it recurred consistently and made her feel extremely uneasy.

The police took her story and experience seriously, and decided to investigate. Since the man paid for everything with a credit card, the police were able to locate the identity and address of this individual. They even set up a stake-out at his residence and for three days, nothing happened. However, on the morning of the third day at around 2 am, the officers observed this man leaving his house. They followed him and pulled him over because he ran a stop sign. They got an uneasy feeling as well and searched the car. When they popped open the trunk, there indeed were his purchases, two large plastic containers, now filled with the concrete. In each plastic tub there was also half of a human body.

I am sorry to recount this horrific story, but it clearly illustrates Donna's use of her intuition after the psychic experience of hearing those words in her mind. Because she trusted her guidance, the police were able to uncover a terrible crime—perhaps forestalling a repeat performance as well.

Develop your psychic sensitivity and gifts. These gifts are a part of your natural abilities that can guide, guard and even protect you.

Your intuitive ability comes over time. Intuition speaks to the greater picture of what is being shown to you. It is your openness to being one with yourself and to tap into the guidance of your spiritual team, whether it is God, angels, spirit guides or Ascended Masters. Intuition is a blend of your awareness, psychic phenomena and connecting with a higher source to receive information, guidance and wisdom.

A Guidebook For Advanced Angel Readings

ASSEMBLE YOUR SPIRITUAL TEAM

In this section, let's explore the angelic realm in more depth and talk about some of the other Light Beings you can also work with during your readings.

There are nine orders in the celestial hierarchy, each with their own unique functions and duties. They are listed below from the highest rank to the lowest. Brief descriptions are included along with their areas of service.

FIRST TIER: SERAPHIM, CHERUBIM, THRONES

Seraphim

Sometimes called the "Burning Ones" because they are the closest to God, the Seraphim comprise the highest order of angels in the angelic realm. They have six wings and surround the throne of God, incessantly singing, "Holy, Holy, Holy." Their name means "Fire Maker" and their job is to remind us of God's glory and love. The Seraphim can purify us with burning love for God. The angelic rulers of the Seraphim include: *Metatron, Michael, Seraphiel, Jehoel* and *Satan* before his fall.

Cherubim

This name means, "Full of Knowledge." Cherubim are called the Recorders and Rulers of the North, South, East and West. Sometimes they are referred to as the voices of Divine wisdom. Their task is to ensure that the universal laws are kept and to protect and defend the throne of God. The angels of the Cherubim include: *Gabriel, Cherubiel, Raphael, Zophiel, Ophaniel and Satan before his fall.*

Thrones

These angels are just below the Seraphim and Cherubim. They are usually portrayed as fiery wheels with wings and many eyes. Some also depict the Thrones as angels that carry the scales of justice and balance. They hold the power of judgment and their job is to contemplate the disposition of Divine justice according to the laws of the universe and God's Will. The Thrones ensure that Divine justice is dispensed in all situations and they maintain cosmic harmony. They are the peacemakers who help to bridge the gap between the visible and invisible worlds. The angelic chiefs of this realm are: *Oriphiel, Zaphkiel or Zabkiel, Jophiel and Raziel.*

SECOND TIER: DOMINIONS, VIRTUES, POWERS

Dominions

Their name means "The Oldest Angel" and they are governed by the first tier of angels. The Dominion's task and responsibility is to supervise the duties of the more junior angels. It is their duty to ensure that everything in the universe moves in accordance with the universal laws. Angels in this category include: *Zadkiel, Hashmal, Zacharael and Muriel.*

Virtues

Often called "The Brilliant Ones," these angels are very bright and radiant. Their function includes organizing and overseeing miracles as well as imparting grace and courage to people who have forgotten who they really are. The Virtues also assist with healing and are said to be the angels that impart the gift of grace and valor to others. The ruling angels here are: *Haniel, Gabriel, Michael and Raphael to name only a few.*

Powers

The Powers look after the Divine plan and sees that order is imposed on the heavenly pathways. They can fight off evil/negative spirits and energies. They can give us strength to stand up for ourselves and help resolve unpleasant situations. The angel rulers of the Powers are: *Chamuel, Camael, Gabriel, Verchiel and Samael.*

THIRD TIER: PRINCIPALITIES, ARCHANGELS, ANGELS

Principalities

These angels are heaven's executive guardians, angelic rulers and protector of nations. They also protect religion and religious leaders, the spirituality of the world and work with other angels, including our guardian angels, to encourage us. The angels in charge include: *Haniel, Requel, Cerviel and Amael.*

Archangels

The managers and supervisors of the guardian angels, these angels are more powerful and larger in size. Sometimes they are referred to as the "Ruling Angels." They can be with everyone at the same time because they are not restricted to time or space. There is an infinite number of Archangels that specialize in a specific human condition, helping to direct the Will of God and ensuring that God's Will is done with perfection.

Angels

There are many angels that are available to assist humanity in our day-to-day activities. Everyone and everything is looked over by angels. Under this category, there are guardian angels, warrior angels and specialty angels.

Now let's look at these sub-categories:

Guardian Angels

These angels are the closest to all human beings. God assigns angels to each human at birth and they stay with us until we transition back home. Our guardian angels have names, personalities and possess intelligence. Their duty is to watch over us and they always know what is best for us. They know us better than we know ourselves, for they have fostered our growth and evolution throughout our lives. A guardian angel's mission is to use this special knowledge of their charge to provide the basic support and guidance needed to lead a healthy, successful, and harmonious life.

Warrior Angels

Warrior angels are big and tall and look like linebackers! They are usually male and they come in pairs (like guards). Their purpose is to be an advocate, championing the causes of underdogs and those who need help. These angels give their charges protection, courage and guard them against toxic environments while initiating change.

Specialty Angels

Like human beings, most angels specialize in performing specific kinds of jobs and tasks so that they can better help people achieve their goals in key areas of life. These angelic specialists include romance angels, employment angels, dream angels, money angels, music angels, health angels, home-finder angels, friendship angels, and hundreds of others to aid you in achieving your desires and goals.

Another branch in the celestial hierarchy is the domain of the Ascended Masters and Saints, Spirit Guides, Ancestral Guides and Power Animals who are available to assist us with our spiritual mastery and soul mission.

Ascended Masters/Saints

The new age term "Ascended Masters" means "coming into awakening with God." The Masters and Saints have fulfilled their Divine plan as great leaders, teachers, and healers here on Earth, and have ascended into the presence of the Divine. They are now in a heavenly dimension where they are able to help everyone who needs them. Each Master has chosen a dominant energetic quality to infuse into their presence and range of experience and expertise. These Masters are available for love, guidance, support, information, answers, and can act as our own personal spiritual mentor. Like God and the angels, these Masters and Saints will never violate our free will. They await our decision to call on them, and at that instant they are with us. They have the ability to be with everyone who calls on them simultaneously, for as Jesus promised, "I am with you always."

Spirit Guides

The term "spirit guide" generally makes reference to one or more entities that watch over, protect, teach, heal, and guide you on your spiritual awakening and journey. In general, spirit guides come to you for a specific reason. According to theosophical doctrine, a spirit guide is a person who has lived many former lifetimes, paid their karmic debts and has advanced beyond a need to reincarnate. There is a general consensus that spirit guides are chosen on "the other side" by human beings who are ready to reincarnate and want their assistance.

Ancestral Guides

An ancestral guide is one who can claim some sort of kinship with you, such as a deceased family member. These ancestral guides can act in the capacity of a guardian angel, surrounding us with love and whispering guidance in our ears, and can bring many gifts to our lives. Most of these guides are great-grandparents, grand-parents, siblings, beloved friends, and parents. Having crossed over, these souls then receive special training in the afterlife about how to become an ancestral guide. Their time on Earth is devoted to gently supporting and guiding family members through life.

Power Animals

According to many shamans, power animals are spirit guides in animal form. The indigenous people of the world believe that animal spirit guides help them with all aspects of life, especially with protection, discernment, guidance and healing. Usually a power animal chooses you, but you can call in certain animal spirit guides that can assist you with a particular project or situation in which you find yourself.

Nature Spirits

Also referred to as fairies and elemental beings, the nature spirits are immortal earth angels whose job is to oversee the life cycle of the plants and animals. They are powerful manifestors and healers and can offer guidance and healing to those who call on them. Unlike the angels, fairies do have bodies and wings, and hold a different vibration. Most are small in size but can be as large as six feet tall. Call on them when you are working with manifestation, in nature or for the environment, or if you need assistance with a pet.

This section introduced you to the various beings in the celestial realms. All you need to do is set the intention of connecting with these powerful beings that support the agenda of Earth and your spiritual growth and ascension.

PENDULUM

What is a pendulum? Simply speaking, it is any weighted suspended object. In radiesthesia, also known as dowsing, it is employed as a tool for sensing energy radiations, which facilitates communication with spirit, as well as divination work such as finding water, buried treasure, a lost item, and map dowsing. Further, pendulums can be used to assist with finding the location of a disease and in the diagnosis of a medical condition. Please note that this must only be done in addition to consultations with health professionals.

Pendulum work can provide "yes/no" responses in a variety of situations, and there are also books and charts that provide methods of divining more complex responses with a simple pendulum!

Working with pendulums dates back to ancient civilization, and became quite popular in the twentieth century, perhaps because it is truly an easy tool to work with, although it does require practice. It is also quite easy to make a pendulum yourself with a ring, pendant, crystal, or any object that is suitably heavy, suspended from string or a chain. Of course there are also many different types available for purchase, made of wood, metal and crystals.

If or when you choose to purchase one, the selection of the right pendulum to work with is very much an individual thing. Personally, I believe that the pendulum chooses you. When I first went shopping for a pendulum, I went through 25 of them before I found one that wanted to work with me.

Whatever type of pendulum you procure, self-made or purchased, make certain it can dangle and swing freely.

It is believed that pendulums work with energy. Based on the principle that everything is energy, a pendulum can pick up on that energy much like an antennae and act as a pointer or indicator of that energy. For more detailed information on working with a pendulum, you may want to take a dowsing class and just practice. For the purpose of this chapter, I will include an effortless way to work with your pendulum.

If you have never tried pendulum work, here is a basic process to follow:

1. Clear your space, and bless your pendulum by any method that is meaningful and effective for you. As with all objects, it holds energy–all sorts of energy and it is best to clear that energy from the pendulum at the beginning of each dowsing session.

2. Gently but firmly hold the pendulum chain or string with your thumb and forefinger of your dominant hand, keeping your arm and body relaxed.

3. Next, you will need to determine what is your "yes" and "no" response. Ask the pendulum to show you a "yes" then ask that it show a "no." Next, test these responses.

This is done by posing questions with answers you already know. For my "yes," the pendulum moves in a clock-wise circle. My "no" is a side-to-side motion.

Once you are completely comfortable that you have calibrated the responses, you are ready to begin.

Formulate your question, keeping in mind that you must be detached from the outcome. If not, you could potentially influence or bias the pendulum's response.

As with your angel readings, the more specific your question, the better! A good example is, "Is it for my highest good and the good of all concerned to change jobs within the next three months?" An example of an improperly worded question would be:

> *"Is it for my highest good and the good of all concerned to either stay in my current job or change jobs?"*

Why is this a badly worded question? Because it is two questions in one and you cannot get a yes/no response.

Within the realms of metaphysics and spirituality, some also employ pendulum work for conducting communication with the spirit world including angels, guides, Ascended Masters or deceased loved ones. In paranormal investigations, it can be used for validating the presence of paranormal activity such as ghosts or earthbound spirits.

Everything has a place and there is a place for everything, and pendulum work during your angel readings is quite acceptable.

I like to use pendulums for chakra dowsing and for map work. When I teach Reiki and psychic development classes, I discuss the belief that we are energy and that we can control our energy, and use the pendulum as a way to illustrate this. After asking for a volunteer, I set the intention of working with that person's energy. Then I hold the pendulum about three to four inches over a particular chakra and ask, "Is Mary's root chakra open?" I wait to get my yes/no response and then ask, "Show me the size of Mary's root chakra." If the pendulum swings very wide (more than four inches), her root chakra is too big. If the pendulum swings very narrow (less than three inches), that indicates that her root chakra is out of balance and too small. A normal chakra center is between three to four inches in diameter.

Now the fun stuff can begin!

When the pendulum indicates that a chakra is out of balance, I suggest to the person I'm working with that they visualize the chakra as perfectly aligned and balanced and that they silently command it to open, align and balance now. Once the person gives their command, it can seem like magic to observe the pendulum adjusting with the energy as the chakra returns to balance. Yes, it is just that easy!

Regarding map dowsing, it too can be a fun and interesting visual tool. When I have a client who is questioning whether it is the right time to make a residential move, I call on my angelic team for guidance on this question. I inquire about the best place for them to relocate to, and if I intuit that this person has many different options, I work with the angels, my world map and the pendulum. The angels will work with whatever tool you wish to work with. In instances of moving, I find that map dowsing with the angels is a perfect match.

You can also use a pendulum or dowsing rods or sticks to find people or especially, one of my favorite things, to find the angels and fairies. Try calling in your guardian angels and ask them to move in close to you. With your pendulum in hand, begin to seek out where they are. The pendulum will pick up on their energy and you will discover their location.

You will likely discover your own favorite ways to work with this tool–try it and see. With practice, pendulum work can be accurate, interesting and fun!

MEDIUMSHIP

Everyone is psychic, but not everyone is a natural medium. A medium is a person who has an ability to connect with the spirit world and receive messages and information from people who have crossed over.

A natural-born medium is an individual who usually at a very young age begins seeing, hearing and feeling spirits. This also includes hearing their name being called although no one appears to be around. Many natural mediums are wide open psychically, meaning that most if not all of their psychic "clairs" are open and expanded.

One way to understand mediumship is to think of a building superintendent. This person has a universal key that unlocks every single door in the whole building complex. Like the superintendent, a natural medium holds a universal key or energy that allows them to work with many different types of energy.

Those who are not born mediums can learn to conduct mediumship sessions. Because they hold a very particular key or energy, they can still unlock and open some of the doors, although perhaps not all of the doors.

I am not a natural medium, yet mediumship frequently occurs during my angel sessions. Deceased loved ones who want to connect with my client through me need to be of a similar energy, one that is congruent with mine, which can align perfectly with my vibration. If an energetic field between us can be created that is of a matching vibration, then the information flowing from the deceased spirit becomes strong, steady and consistent.

In some instances, if a deceased loved one has a message and wishes to connect or be a part of the session, but cannot work with the reader's energy, there may be another spirit that is willing to come in and act as a connector.

For example, during one session, there was a grandfather who wanted to speak with his granddaughter, but our energies would not work together. So the grandfather brought in another deceased family member who acted as an energy link to me. Through this spirit, they communicated the information and messages to me, and my client was able to connect with her grandfather.

Now let's talk about the mediumship process and how all this works.

Mediumship uses of all of your "clairs" (clairaudience, claircognizance, clairsentience and clairvoyance). For more details on each "clair," please refer to my book, *Angel Readings for Beginners*.

At the start of your session, ALWAYS invoke Archangel Michael to create sacred, holy and protected space, and say a prayer of protection. Michael is the protector and can act as a spirit bouncer or gatekeeper, only allowing the appropriate spirit into the session that is for your client's highest good and highest healing.

Quite often the deceased loved one already knows ahead of time about the upcoming session. They may help to arrange it and even appear "early" for it because they are really excited about making contact. They will most likely come right through clearly and easily!

After creating your sacred space, begin with sensing spirits around your client. Just close your eyes and take a few deep and slow breaths. Allow your mind to relax and slowly focus your attention around the area of your client's shoulders. Try to discern if there are any differences in this area. When you get the feeling that one shoulder has "something" different around it, focus on the energy around that area. Now focus on the type of energy that is next to your client (feminine or masculine energy). Ask the spirit to validate who they are and what messages do they want to give to your client.

If you do not sense anyone around your client, be honest. Because of other projects or tasks that they are working on, not all spirits are available. In some instances due to unresolved guilt, the deceased loved one may be reluctant about showing up. In cases where you do not sense anyone, and the client wishes to communicate with a particular family member or friend, you can ask Archangel Michael and the angels to assist.

To invite a deceased loved one into the sacred space, ask your client for the first name of the person with whom they wish to connect. Ask your client hold in their mind's eye or their imagination a mental picture of that deceased person. Then, invoke Archangel Michael to locate this spirit and to bring them into the reading. Request that the spirit validate their presence and identity, and if your client wants to ask a question, they may do so. You can even instruct the deceased loved one to communicate messages and information via the angel cards. It works!

This type of spirit connection proves to be quite healing for the client. Remember, trust what you get and use discernment when relaying information to your client.

The C.E.R.T. method is the most well-known format among mediums. The formula was developed by international psychic medium, author and therapist Steven O'Brien of Swansea, UK.

C.E.R.T. stands for Communicator, Evidence, Reason and Tie It Up.

Communicator

> Who is communicating with you? Is this spirit male or female? Are they a friend, immediate family member or some type of other relative? Also, try to assess the personality of the communicator. Are they quiet or shy or out-spoken and talkative? Pay attention to everything.

Evidence

> This means receiving evidence from the communicator. Ask the deceased spirit to provide some tangible evidence

that is related to whom they are. Inquire about objects, memories or a description of something (like their home or a special childhood toy or even some jewelry) that they valued and held close to their heart. Let them provide all specific details, which the client will be able to validate.

Reason

Ask the spirit why have they returned? What message(s) or information do they want to share with you for your client? Once again: Pay attention to everything that you get and TRUST.

Tie It Up

This is where you conclude your reading and pull every-thing together. Many times the deceased spirit will communicate a message or symbol of love such as a pink or red rose to indicate their love and support.

When your mediumship session concludes, give thanks to all those in the angelic realm and spirit world for assisting you with your reading. Then clear your aura, clean your chakras and detach all energy cords.

Mediumship can be a very powerful tool for healing. Some of the benefits of mediumship include:

- Assists your client in healing from grief, guilt, regret or other emotional distress.

- Helps both the deceased spirit and your client to release each other so that they can continue with their spiritual progress. If the survivor's guilt/sadness is strong, it can keep the deceased loved one earthbound.

- Lets your client know that their loved one did survive death and that they are doing quite well.

- Helps in overcoming the fear of physical death.

One last note: Just because a loved one is in spirit now, it does not automatically mean that they are spiritually evolved or enlightened. They still have their egos intact. So, trust what you receive and use discernment when relaying messages and information to your client.

CHANNELING

Everyone can be a channeler even though you may not be conscious or aware of this wonderful and powerful gift.

Channeling is the ability to receive thought forms from the higher realms of Light. These thought forms can be translated into messages of love, healing, information and Divine guidance. Through the channeling process, the channeler receives and relays messages and information.

Channeling is one method of communicating with angels, Ascended Masters, spirit guides, Higher Self, God, deceased loved ones and non-physical entities.

Historically, channeling emerged out of the séance rage of the early 20th century. People had a fascination with contacting deceased loved ones and this gave way to the birth of channeling.

Divination and healing, as well as possession are also forms of channeling.

There are different types of channeling that range from full conscious to full trance.

In full conscious channeling, the channeler is fully aware of the energies and retains memory of what they channeled.

With trance channeling, the channeler allows the spirit or energy to take full control over their body, allowing the spirit to speak through them directly.

Another type of channeling is connecting with spirit in a meditative state. Automatic writing is an additional method whereby the person connects and receives messages through a stream of consciousness that is more personal in nature. We will cover automatic writing in Chapter 9.

In order to channel or to be a channel, you need to understand energy and how to direct that energy. Remember, everything is energy, energy is everything and each energy has its own unique frequency.

In channeling, you are the receiver. You are like that old radio dial in the cars. When one channels, they are tapping or plugging into the frequency of a particular energy. It's like plugging into a switchboard and connecting with someone at the other end. If, for example, you would like to channel Archangel Michael, simply tune into his frequency signature and listen. Channeling involves raising your vibration and adjusting your frequency to match the energy frequency of whomever you wish to channel.

In learning how to channel, you will need to raise your vibration and increase your own energy. Meditation, breath work, yoga and prayer are a few ways in which you can increase your energy and vibration. You can also just call in the energy of the universe. See the universal life flow energy all around and invite it in. Focus on your breath.

After you become confident in your ability to call in the energy, you can begin to channel.

The process of channeling is simple yet it does take practice and focus. Here is an easy step-by-step process for you to begin channeling.

- Set your intention to channel and establish who you want to connect with.

- Call in Archangel Michael to surround you and to guide, guard, and protect you while channeling.

- Breathe and center yourself.

- Call in the energy and visualize your aura expanding and the energy filling you and the entire room or space that you are in.

- Allow your mind to wander (no thoughts, just allow).

- Be specific when you call forth the being/energy/ entity you want to connect with. If you are too general, you may get someone or something you really did not want.

- Be open to all messages. You may wish to record them, have a friend take notes, or use a dictaphone.

- Trust what you receive and do not edit.

❥ When finished, remember to say "Thank you," disconnect from the energy and clear yourself.

When channeling, always be humble and grateful. Always have purity of heart and the desire to serve.

AKASHIC RECORDS

According to *Element Encyclopedia of the Psychic World*, the word "Akashic" is a Sanskrit word that means "fundamental etheric substance of the universe." The Akashic Record is therefore a perfect and complete energetic archive of all human experience, and more. They are also referred to as "Soul Records," "Book of Life," "Library of Life," "Lamb's Book of Life," "Library of Light" and the "Book of God's Remembrance."

It has been said that many ancient people around the world, including the Tibetans, Egyptians, Persians, Greeks, Chinese, Hebrews, Christians, Druids, and Mayans knew of the existence of the Akashic Records. In fact, many ancient sacred texts such as the Old and New Testament make reference to the Akashic Records. In the Old Testament (Psalm 69:28) and the New Testament (Philippians 4:3, Revelation 3:5, 13:8, 17:8, 20:12, 20:15 and 21:27), the Akashic Records are referred to as the Book of Life. In Egypt, those who could read the Akashic Records were held in high standing and were often found advising Pharaohs.

The Akashic Records can be equated to a central storehouse of all information for every person who has ever lived on Earth.

The records chronicle every word, feeling, thought, action and intent that has ever occurred in the world, storing all of this information like a cosmic computer.

There is a group of beings which some refer to as the "Collective Keepers" or the "Lords of the Akashic Records" who are overseen by Archangel Metatron. These Beings of Light ensure that our records are safe and secure, and that the information recorded is true and accurate.

According to Edgar Cayce, if we can achieve a superconscious level, we can access the Akashic Record, which is like visiting an enormous library and looking up information.

Consulting a person's Akashic Records during a reading can be very enlightening, even life changing, as it adds new insights from past lives to the present.

Some of the benefits of accessing the records include: understanding and balancing karma, relationships of past and present lifetimes and soul lessons.

Here is a very simple way to conduct an Akashic Record reading for your client.

❥ Before you begin the reading, ask your client for their legal birth name and any nicknames they happen to use. Why? Because your name holds your identity and your vibration, it acts much like a key that will open a specific door, the door to your Akashic Record.

❥ Next, create sacred and protective space around yourself and your client. Ask God to create a pyramid of Light all around you. Then invoke the four mighty Archangels: Michael for discernment and protection, Gabriel for truth, Raphael for health and healing and Uriel to help you access a higher consciousness through your mind's eye.

⬥ Breathe and be centered and still.

⬥ Call forth the presence of Archangel Metatron to be with you. Let him know your intention for conducting an Akashic Record reading and ask him to safely guide you to the Hall of Records for your client or even for yourself.

⬥ Ask your client by name for permission to open their records. Then have them close their eyes, help them to relax perhaps by speaking to them quietly and have them take a few slow deep breaths.

⬥ While their eyes are closed, silently to yourself, read the following:

> "I ask God, the Universal Source, to place a permanent shield of Love and Truth around (*say client's name*) and me, so that only God's universal love and truth will exist between (*say client's name*) and me.
>
> I allow the Masters, angels, teachers, and loved ones of (*say client's name*) to channel through me out of whatever realms to say whatever is of purpose and useful.

I ask that all necessary knowledge and information needed for this reading be forced through my subtle bodies and auric field now.

I ask the permission of the Lords of the Akashic Records to enter the Hall of Records and to access the records of (*say client's name*) and remove whatever information that is useful and necessary for this reading."

Now you will be able to proceed with the reading, and when the reading is done, seal the records by saying "Thank you and AMEN."

How you receive and experience the records depend on how you process the energy and information. You may actually see the record book with the information or receive an intuitive download depending on which "clair" is the strongest for the reader.

In essence, accessing our Akashic Records can reveal new understanding and wisdom of ourselves and shift or change our own consciousness, awakening us to a deeper level of who we truly are. Always approach the process with trust, as well as with great reverence for the information revealed to you. Whatever you learn must only be used for your client's understanding and growth, and as with all aspects of every reading, must be kept completely confidential.

OTHER TOOLS FOR YOUR READINGS

In this chapter we are going to explore additional ways that you can deepen your angel readings. While all readings are a wonderful and easy way to start a dialogue with your angelic team, here you will find suggestions for a few other new tools that you can explore.

Hopefully by now you have created for yourself a regular daily routine of spiritual hygiene, like clearing your aura, cleaning your chakras, dissolving psychic etheric cords and shielding. If not, you may want to consider doing this. It will make your spiritual connection stronger and your angel readings clearer. This is therefore an essential foundation tool.

Now, let's see what else you might add to your toolbox.

Altars: Creating Sacred Space

In the space where you are planning to conduct your readings, you may want to create an angel alter. Creating an alter helps to establish your sacred space and sanctuary. It is a tangible focal point for your readings, which creates an atmosphere of serenity for both you and your client.

Some suggested items for your angel alter are objects sacred to your belief system, such as angel statues, incense, photos of Ascended Masters and angels, candles, crystals, tokens of love and endearment that you have received from the angels, and other items that have sacred meaning to you. When you look at these things, your heart opens, you feel safe and comfortable, and you are able to achieve a meditative state more easily.

When preparing for an angel reading session, first set your intention of doing a reading, invoke Archangel Michael directing him to clear you, your reading space and all things within it including your angel cards. Ask Michael to create a ring of violet fire around you and your client in which the violet flame provides holy, sacred and protected space for your reading, even if the reading is done by phone or internet.

Invocation: Assembling the Perfect Energies

Usually, when you begin a reading, you bring in your angel team, which may include Archangel Michael, guardian angels and perhaps a few other archangels that you feel close to or even your spirit guide. Well, instead of trying to either bring in everyone or just a few chosen ones, how about bringing in the enlightened beings that would be most appropriate for that person and reading? Doesn't that sound appealing? All right, it is easy to do! Here is what I say when I am preparing for a reading, whether it is for one person that day or for multiple readings.

"Archangel Michael, please be with me now

and clear me, the oracle cards and the space in which I am conducting the readings for the day. Extend your protective energy all around me. I now call forth the energy of God, the Divine Source of All, to dwell deep within me, creating holy, sacred and protected space within me and all around me and assisting me in being the perfect Divine tool and messenger for these readings today.

I ask my personal team to assemble, including my guardian angels and spirit guides. I call forth all of the angels, archangels, guides, Masters and deceased loved ones who have the most beneficial and appropriate messages, information and guidance for those whom I am doing readings for today. I also ask that everyone's reading is for their highest good, healing and purpose. Thank you!"

Now this takes the guesswork out of figuring out which angels, guides, and Masters are supposed to be working with me. You can use this or any variation that feels right to you.

Calibration: Keeping Divination Objects Clean and Clear

At times, you may have experienced laying out cards and they just don't seem right. They may even have a funny feel to them and the messages from the cards do not seem to fit or be appropriate. This means it's time to check on the energy and accuracy of your reading cards, or any other objects you use in your readings.

Remember, everything is energy, and that energy surrounds us and everything in our environment, including our physical divination tools.

Here's an example of how I check the accuracy my oracle cards: First I ask God, the Divine Source of All, to connect directly with me and to work through me with the cards. I then program my cards for a "yes" and "no" response. If you do not know how to program your cards, you will find a simple method in my *Angel Readings for Beginners* book.

Then I ask God, "God do you love me?" If my cards are clear, clean and calibrated to my energy, then the "yes" card should come right up. Why? It is my belief that God is 100% pure Love. As long as you hold this belief, this method will prove extremely useful. If you receive a "no," then ask God to clear the cards. When in doubt ask God! Again, you are of course free to use as written, or to formulate this question using whatever words hold meaning for you.

Automatic Writing: Journaling with the Divine

Another tool that is simple and powerful is automatic writing and creating an angel journal. Automatic writing is a stream of consciousness writing that comes from being in an altered state of consciousness. It is another way in which channeling can occur. Some like to use this tool as a way to receive messages from the angels, guides, Masters, deceased loved ones and other inter-dimensional Beings of Light.

When exploring automatic writing, you can use paper and pen or even type on a computer. The words you record are frequently words you would not normally use or the messages are communicated in a language style that is not normal for you.

When venturing into automatic writing, following a procedure or protocol will make for an easier, productive and positive experience.

Here are the steps that I use to practice automatic writing, this is only an example of an automatic writing session with your guardian angels.

1. Assemble your angelic team by calling on Archangel Michael and your guardian angels. Let them know your intention of doing an automatic writing session with them and set up your angel appointment. So you could say, "Archangel Michael and my guardian angels please be with me now. I want to schedule an automatic writing session with you today at 2 pm and I will see you back here today at 2 pm. Thank you." By setting up a session, you are telling them your intention and giving them as well as yourself time to prepare.

2. The angels are never late so make sure you are on time.

3. Place yourself in a comfortable position, perhaps sitting in your meditation space or on a couch or chair with pen and paper in hand or computer in your lap.

4. Call on Archangel Michael, asking him to create a circle of protection all around you and to oversee your automatic writing session.

5. Next, call in your guardian angels and ask them to connect with your physical energy.

6. Take a few deep breaths, relax your physical body and allow your mind to be open and wander.

7. With pen in hand, rest your hand comfortably on the paper, or keyboard if you happen to be using a computer, and begin to write either a very specific question or simply write, "Dear Angels, what do I need to know right now?"

8. Be patient and allow the angels to write through you. Trust what you are receiving.

9. Release the urge to sensor, judge or doubt. Your whole angelic team is right there beside you. They want to make that connection with you as much as you do.

10. Now one of two things may happen. Some may receive a download of what the message is or what they need to write. If you deeply trust the angels physically connecting with you, they will take hold of the pen and physically move your hand and write through you. At first it may just be a lot of scribbles because they are not used to your denser energy, but over time, the writing will smooth out and you can read clear messages from your heavenly team.

11. When your session feels complete or the angels say, "That is enough for now," thank the angels for their love, guidance and wisdom. When you are ready, read the message that they gave you and reflect on the meaning of the message.

Psychometry: Energy Impressions

Have you either heard of psychometry or tried it? The term "psychometry" was coined back in the 1800's by Joseph Buchanan and the term is derived from the Greek word, "psyche," which means "soul" and "metron"which means to "measure."

Simply speaking, psychometry is divining knowledge and information from an object about a person that is connected with that object.

Remember, objects hold energy and psychometry is the means by which you can read the energy off that object. Using your psychic gifts, you can intuit events and emotions past, present and future connected to the object by physically holding it.

The best objects to read are personal items, especially those that are handled only by one person, such as a piece of jewelry, car keys, photos, etc.

Psychometry uses all of your "clairs," which in this instance are triggered by the sense of touch as you hold the object that you are reading. Here is an easy and simple way to try psychometry to see if it is a tool that you would like to use during your readings.

> ⟩ First, have your client select an item that they are wearing or have brought with them which is significant in their life.

> ⟩ Next, as you hold the object between your hands, center yourself, breathe, and allow your mind to wander and be free. You may also find it useful to receive and hold the object only in the hand that is non-dominant. Your dominant hand is usually the one you send energy with, so it may be easier to perform psychometry with the other or receptive hand.

> ⟩ Then you'll begin to get pictures or impressions. Trust what you get and share the information as it comes to you. The person for whom you are reading may take notes and record any information and impressions that you are receiving. Request feedback only when you are done.

With perseverance and honest feedback from your subject, you will find that your skill at psychometry quickly improves.

Some of the tools I have described above take practice and patience, while some are simply a matter of you're choosing to utilize them. Even so, they all work best when you have a sense of sacred trust and respect for your own ability, as well as for your Divine support.

You may want to work with your angelic team and ask them to assist you in developing some unique angel healing techniques for both your own use, and in your readings for others.

LOOKING FOR EARTH ANGELS

I n this chapter we will talk about "Earth Angels," discuss how to discover whether your client is one, and if so, what type, as well as how this information can be useful to them.

Everyone has a personal soul mission, which encompasses our life lessons. These are the things we agreed to learn and possibly master during a particular incarnation. Earth Angels however, have an additional responsibility. Along with their personal soul mission, they also have a global soul mission to help make a difference on Earth, which may include working for the masses and the multitudes.

In essence, this means that their contract includes elevating the condition of humanity, the planet, or the animal kingdom in some way. Sometimes, it's even a combination of all of the above! Many Earth Angels do feel "different," as they sense that they are here for a purpose beyond learning life lessons.

Most Earth Angels feel like they do not fit in and often have a challenging time with the energies of this great big schoolhouse called Earth.

While I was originally taught that there are five types of Earth Angels, I have since discovered two more categories. So there are at least seven different types of Earth Angels, and while not all Earth Angels have them, there are also seven different types of wings. Yes, wings!

The first time I heard about people having wings, I just had to laugh and did not believe it was possible. Then the angels decided to give me an unforgettable experience, which made me a true believer.

This happened not long after I had completed my angel training and was still working in the biotech field. One afternoon, while I was speaking with a friend who worked in the Human Resource department, an HR colleague of hers came into her office for assistance with a work-related matter. Respecting this, I attempted to excuse myself and leave the room but Shannon, my friend, insisted I stay. So I sat back in my chair and zoned out since I was not part of their brief conversation. I happened to be gazing at the general area around my friend's shoulder and within two minutes, there they were...wings. Yes, big angel wings! I could see very clearly with my physical eyes an outline of white energy in the shape of angel wings. I shouted to my friend, "Shannon you have wings!?" She stopped her conversation, looked at me and with a very serious face and said, "Yes, I know," and then returned to her previous conversation. My friend had angel wings. Amazing and cool!

That was my first experience of actually seeing wings. Now that I know where to look and how to scan for wings, it seems as though virtually everyone who comes to me for a reading or a class is some type of Earth Angel! I hardly ever get a mortal–you know, a regular person–for a reading.

There are feathery angel wings of the type commonly depicted in paintings, butterfly wings, dragonfly wings, angel wings with a watery feel or the sense of a body of water around the person, dragon wings and Pegasus wings. Some individuals also have the marking of the unicorn horn on their forehead.

Those who can see or sense wings may perceive them in different translucent or solid colors. As previously noted, not all Earth Angels have wings, yet they hold a very specific type of energy which can be felt even though wings are not sensed.

Now let's explore the different types of Earth Angels.

Incarnated Angels

The individuals in this category are from the angelic realm and usually have angel wings that you can see with either your physical eyes or your mind's eye. I have found that Lightworkers in this category tend to look like angels with more rounded faces and some have gentle dispositions. Often they are employed in some type of service work, have a difficult time saying "no" and struggle with boundaries. Incarnated angels frequently attract inappropriate partners because they see the best potential in everyone and tend to want to make everyone happy, even at their own expense.

Incarnated Elementals

These individuals are strongly connected to the Earth, nature and the fairy realm, and some are connected to water. They are powerful healers and manifestors, more so than the average person. Quite a few Incarnated Elementals have wings, such as butterfly wings, dragonfly wings, Pegasus wings or angel wings that either have water around them or have a water vibration around them. Only a few have the marking of the unicorn on their forehead.

Are you familiar with the old saying, "Be careful what you wish for, you may end up getting it?" Well for the Incarnated Elementals, since they can manifest whatever they want in a very short amount of time, they would be wise to learn how to harness their power and use it in a positive and productive manner. I have also discovered in working with Incarnated Elementals that they have the toughest time being here on planet Earth. They struggle with self-esteem or self-worth and are more prone to depression, addiction, and trust issues.

Wise Ones

Another category includes individuals who are reincarnated shamans, alchemists and mystics. The Wise Ones are more in tune with their psychic gifts and usually love to dabble in Wicca, witchcraft, mysticism, astrology and shamanism. These individuals usually gravitate toward psychic readings, intuitive healing work and spiritual teaching. Only a few have dragon wings.

Walk-Ins

A comparatively small number of individuals belong to this category. A Walk-In entails a soul-to-soul exchange, in which a more highly evolved soul wishes to bypass the regular method of incarnating in physical form. For many, there is a soul exchange agreement either prior to incarnating or during some period of the present lifetime. This is a free-will agreement by both souls made in Divine order and is not to be confused with spirit possession.

The soul exchange can happen during a surgery, accident or even a meditation. The Walk-Ins that I have encountered usually change every aspect of their lives, including their name, job and friends. They may even relocate and take on a whole new image and persona.

Star People

These are wonderful souls who tend to be gentle, kind, patient and very forgiving. They do not like being in the limelight and though many enter healing professions, they are more noted for being the peacemakers. If a star person has only incarnated a few times, they may appear to be socially inappropriate, not knowing how to act, feel or interact with others. Also, many Star People have an unusual aura, more rainbow color energy around them.

Goddesses

These are individuals who hold Goddess or High Priestess energy. For the Goddesses, truth, integrity and beauty are what they hold deep within their heart and mind. Independent and strong-willed, many even have the features of very feminine, beautiful women. Some have in past incarnations served alongside Pallas Athena, also known as Goddess Athena, in the Temple of Truth and Wisdom.

Divine Ones

These individuals are far and few between. Their energy is pure and they have an open heart, truly possessing unconditional love. They hold Divine Love within them and they practice it. When you encounter such an individual, it is like being in the presence of an Ascended Master. You may also notice that their heart chakra is pink.

To scan for wings on a client, first hold the thought and intention. Next, soften your vision and slowly scan about their shoulders, sides and back for wings. If you feel more comfortable doing this with your eyes closed, you can. Try to get a sense and feel of the person's energy. Focus your attention on those areas and trust what you get. Try it!

If you perceive that the person you are reading for is an Earth Angel, let your intuition guide you regarding whether you should let them know. As you may have already discovered, not every client is open to the idea of past lives or the various realms. That said, it can be great fun when they are! Sometimes, I even make a game out of this with clients. I notice their wings and explain about Earth Angels and the different types of wings. Then I have them close their eyes, center themselves with slow, rhythmic breathing and tell them where to focus their inner vision. Most of the time they can see or sense their wings! It is rather a fun and unique experience and an empowering one as well, as it builds the client's confidence in their own intuitive abilities.

The ability to identify Earth Angels and their wings can serve both you and your client. If indeed your client seems as if they would be comfortable hearing this information and you do share it with them, the effect can at times be life-changing. For some Earth Angels, it is the first time they realize that they are not alone and feel some sense of belonging. It can be an answer to some of the questions they've had about their preferences and choices, experiences and struggles, strengths and weaknesses. Many are drawn to working with an intuitive of some kind only after searching for understanding in various ways, including formal therapy, with limited success. Recognizing a past life and how it impacts the present can bring acceptance and peace. Change often follows! The change may be small such as keeping more live greenery or a fountain in their home or workspace, or larger like relocating and new career directions. Either way, I have seen this knowledge open the way for more joy and purpose.

There will certainly be times it seems inappropriate to express the idea of being an Earth Angel to the person for whom you are doing a reading. It is still a useful part of the information you receive from the Divine, as it provides insight, guidance and direction which you can convey in some form your client will find easier to accept.

So, look out for those Earth Angels and use or share this knowledge to help others find inner peace, the strength to follow their calling or global soul mission and add joy and fun to their lives.

QUESTIONS & ANSWERS

In this section we will explore several topics of concern that can come up in your angel readings along with possible ways to handle such questions from your clients. Remember that especially when conducting an angel session, it is important to be nonjudgmental and to hold the thought of being the best Divine messenger that you can be.

Here are some special topics and questions from clients. This is only a guideline to assist you, with the understanding that your true guide in every reading is the Divine.

Job Search

> "I have been unemployed for a long time, do you see a new job soon?" or "I am tired of my current job and want to make a change, is anything new coming?"

Because of all the changes happening around us these days, many are very concerned about job stability and being able to make enough money to continue to support themselves and their family. If your client requests information about changing or finding a job, work closely with their guardian angels, but also bring in Archangel Michael, Archangel Gabriel and Saint Joseph (Jesus' father, who worked as a carpenter). Michael can help with removing blocks and obstacles. Gabriel is great at networking, ensuring that a resume ends up on the right person's desk and the whole interview process goes smoothly. St. Joseph works magic in leading the person to all the right companies as well as facilitating the networking process. Your client's guardian angels can also provide you with information about possible new job opportunities coming up or the type of field or area your client can explore.

Finances

> "*When are my finances going to turn around?*" or "*I am so far in debt, can the angels help me?*"

This is another challenging question. We are all personally responsible for our own abundance or the lack thereof. We create everything including our own debt or wealth. So when a client is inquiring about their financial situation, the angels will often come through with some pretty practical guidance and advice.

Remember that money is simply a manifestation of our own energy and nothing else. Many people either fear or hate money. Their own feelings and beliefs can begin to block the flow of financial abundance in their lives.

When finances are brought up in a reading, the angels can have quite a sense of humor and they show me a messy wallet.

So I ask my client to get their wallet and after carefully opening their money section, I frequently find their green cash all mixed up with papers, receipts, coins, credit cards and other things all mixed in together. Once during a "Creating Prosperity with the Angels" class, I asked a lady to give me her wallet. She dove into her huge handbag and pulled out her wallet which I thought would explode in my hands. Not only was it extremely messy, but she also had a suppository mixed in with her money! After you're done laughing, think about the energetic impact. This person held down three jobs just to make ends meet...so money in and money out. It never really stayed around.

If you get the "hit" that your client has a messy wallet, teach them about money. Explore their feelings and beliefs about money. Then show them how to clean up their wallet, treat their money with respect and ask Archangel Michael and Archangel Ariel to heal any negative feelings or beliefs around money and abundance. The angels can best work with us for healing and adjusting our negative self-limiting thoughts when we are asleep. Advise your client to share their concerns with their angels and request healing just before going to sleep. Suggest that they consciously connect with the energy of money when they are paying for something and say, "God, thank you for my prosperity." When receiving money, do the same. Say, "Thank you God, for my abundance from the hard work that I have done." Genuine and heartfelt gratitude opens more doors for abundance to come your way. Make peace with money...it's a translation of our own energy and we all need to appreciate that.

Health

> *"Do you see any health issues coming up for*
> *me?"* or *"I am concerned about my health, do*
> *the angels have anything to say about this?"*

Health is always a touchy subject for many and even for myself at times. When a client asks this type of question, I do two things. First, I ask that the client's astral body step forward and I scan that energy field. Our spiritual body holds information and the potentiality of health issues. If there is a potential medical condition, I see this in my mind's eye written just over their head.

Second, I scan the client's entire body. When I encounter a trouble spot, that area is highlighted in red and I mention to them what I am seeing.

During some readings I have done, deceased family members who have passed away due to a particular health condition have shown up. This is a stronger indication that the client may be headed down the same path and needs to take action and make some health changes.

If I am shown a potential health problem, I may ask if it runs in the family. Regardless of whether it does or not, I will suggest that the client seek out a physical exam or stay on top of the situation. For example, if I see the word "diabetes" over a person's head, I will ask whether diabetes runs in the family or if anyone passed away from complications of diabetes. If "yes" is their response, they usually understand that they need to be more aware and take better care of their body, perhaps via diet or regular check-ups. Should my client say there is no history of diabetes, I will still suggest that the potential for it exists and that they need to be more vigilant about their self-care regimen (healthier eating, exercise, rest and mindful of sugar intake).

Never state that the person has a definite medical condition, make any diagnosis or play doctor unless you are a physician yourself. You can only suggest potential health issues and ask the angels what your client can do to avoid these issues. If your client validates that they do have a particular condition, you can certainly explore this with the help of the angels.

Death and Dying

> *"When am I going to die?"* or *"Will I survive my current health crisis?"*

This is always a tough subject. Can you intuit the death age of a person? Yes, you can. However, I would rather focus on living. One quick note to make here: There is a belief that we all freely choose prior to incarnation at least three ages when we can leave this Earth plane. This all depends on where we are on our soul path and may explain near-death experiences. Having crossed over, a soul may agree to return to complete a project or mission or to fulfill an additional contract. Our thoughts, feelings and beliefs about the afterlife create our experience of the other side. Those who believe in the devil and fire may indeed experience their own personal hell. Yes, this is how it all works!

When I am intuitively told that a person is going to pass, I silently assess my client. I physically observe the person and ask myself, "Can they mentally, emotionally and spiritually handle this information?" Then I ask my spiritual team if it is necessary to share this information. If their response is "Yes," I ask them to work with me using my oracle cards and give a story with the card images and provide me the right words to use. Remember the first rule of thumb, "Do No Harm." When I have done this, the angels have never let me down. I always request and trust my angelic guidance. My advice is that you do the same, share only when guided to.

Romance

> *"When is my soulmate coming?"* or *"Is my love life going to change this year?"*

There are several things to consider when dealing with romantic questions. First you will need to know if the person's most ideal soulmate is here in physical form. If so, this still does not guarantee that they will be together. So you will need to ask if there is potential for these two people meet and become a couple. You must also uncover whether this is truly a soulmate relationship or a soulmate-helpermate relationship. Yes, there is a lot to someone's love life. A soulmate-helpermate is an individual who may or may not belong to your client's soul family, but has agreed to connect with them in this lifetime to fulfill a specific contract. They may want to have a certain experience, or need to learn and master a specific lesson. The relationship is not usually long lasting.

There are times when the ideal soulmate is not on the Earth plane. I do not enjoy these types of readings because I want everyone to have a loving, respectful and fun soulmate.

If the answer is "No," explain this, as well as the fact that fun and romance is perfectly possible, even without a soulmate relationship.

So, if your client has questions about their love life and they want to make changes, here are some questions you can ask. Is the person's heart open or closed? Are they ready to make a commitment to taking action regarding their love life? These are all important questions to explore and discuss. If they are ready to move ahead, here is my Divine prescription for finding their most ideal soulmate or romantic partner.

- Make a decision to change your love life.

- Make a firm commitment to your love life without any hesitation or reservations. Be willing to take action and put energy into it.

- Know what you want and create a list of the qualities and attributes you are looking for in a soulmate. Remember, the universe takes your words and intentions very literally. So, if you are looking for a single male or female, you will need to be specific, otherwise the cosmic joke will be on you. Think about all the people in your life that truly love and support you. What are their qualities and attributes? This will help you to create your list. Since I am a "keep my options open" person, at the very end of your list, you can add, "Dear God, this or something better."

- Create an action plan for making yourself available to others. Try some different activities that are fun or creative. Join a new group; take up a new hobby or class. Just do something different rather than stay at home. If you just work and go home each day, the only person you are most likely to meet is either the mailperson or the Maytag guy. Yes, they may be wonderful–but married. So you decide.

♦ Now partner with spirit to help you in order to manifest. Sit quietly with your list in hand and say out loud, "My guardian angels, romance angels, my Higher Self and Mother Mary, please be with me now." Say it like you mean it. Allow those energies to come in and settle, and explain to them that you are requesting their assistance for your love life. Read your list aloud, describing what you are looking for. They will listen very intently and then work together with you to create the perfect meeting of these soulmates. Yes, it can be that simple, and keep your list until the soulmate or romantic partner manifests.

♦ Trust your Divine guidance as to what you need to do. All of a sudden you may get the message to go to a certain place or call a particular person. Even if it does not make sense, trust and take action. You will be happy that you did.

♦ When your soulmate appears, remember to say "Thank you" to your angelic love counselors!

Sexual Preference

"Do God and my angels hate me because I am gay?" or *"What do the angels have to say about my sexual preferences?"*

In truth, God and angels love each and every one equally regardless of sexual preference, color of skin, financial status or religious beliefs and practices. There is no judgment on their part and neither should there be on ours. Remember, you were made in the image and likeness of the Divine, so how could God not love you?

It has been my experience in working with gay individuals that God and angels truly do not care about someone's sexual preferences. They care only that you honor yourself and your feelings, and that you are with someone who truly and deeply loves you. That is it, simple and true! To pretend to be someone you are not honors no one.

Pregnancy

> *"Am I going to have children?"* or *"What can you tell me about my unborn baby?"*

These are all important and practical questions and need to be dealt with in a delicate manner.

When a client is inquiring about children and most specifically if they will have children in the future, it is best to work with their guardian angels, Archangel Gabriel, Archangel Raphael and Mother Mary. Many times when someone is going to become pregnant, I scan around their head and try to sense a child-like energy or see a little face hovering around the client. However, sensing a child presence around a person does not necessarily mean that they are going to have a child. Instead, it means that there is a potential for pregnancy. It is my belief that it is the soul of the child who determines whether to incarnate or not.

Even if you do not sense or see a child around your client, ask the angels whether or not your client is going to become pregnant. If the answer is "yes," then inquire if the pregnancy will go full-term; depending on this outcome, you can ask further questions. If the answer is "no," ask the angels for any further information they can provide. Perhaps this experience was part of the soul contract, or the body that they chose may not comfortably or safely support childbearing. These are all areas to explore and inquire about. Whatever the outcome is, just reassure your client that it is all in perfect and Divine order.

Addictions

> *"I have a drinking problem and I want to stop,*
> *but can't. Can the angels help me?"*

The answer is always "yes." If this type of question or concern from your client comes up, Archangel Michael and Archangel Raphael are excellent archangels to work with along with the Higher Self of your client. Michael can dissolve energy cords between your client and their particular addiction with his blue flaming sword. Raphael can help heal the body if there is a physical addiction involved. However, when addressing the psychological motivations behind the addiction, it would be best for you to refer to your client to a mental health professional and preferably one that specializes in addictions. I keep a rolodex on hand for readings in case I need to refer a client out.

Now let us focus on potential issues that you may personally encounter while conducting angel sessions.

Needing Validation

> *"How do I know the information I am receiving is accurate and true?"*

We are masters of mistrust so even when we get a strong and clear message, our ego may try to convince us that it is not real. God and angels understand our struggle with trust and truly want us to believe in ourselves, our gifts and the messages that we receive. The angelic hierarchy is very patient and willing to give us validation, but only if we ask for it. Do the best that you can to receive a message, even for yourself. When in doubt, you can call on the angels and ask for validation, either a general sign or a specific sign, and give them a time frame. For example, I personally like receiving validation with numbers. When I am in need of validation for a message or information, I call on my team and say, "Angels, I think you were telling me that my upcoming trip to Bhutan is a go. Please show me three consecutive fours for "yes," and if it is "no," then show me three consecutive nines today."

Be very observant and pay attention to everything throughout your day. Your validation could come via a license plate, receipt, street address, television show or a phone number, just to name a few possibilities.

Asking for confirmation and validation is fine, but please do not become dependent on it. There will come a time when you will simply need to TRUST.

Reading Not Flowing

> *"What should I do if the information is not forthcoming or flowing easily?"*

There are a variety of reasons why your angel sessions may not flow well. It could be that your client may not really want a reading and was pressured by a friend or family member. It may be that you are not the appropriate reader or that an angel reading is not the right type of reading for this person. Another possibility is that you are too tired or that you have some personal issues going on which make it hard for you to connect and be clear.

If for any reason your reading session is not flowing, then quite simply stop it. Refund the money and refer elsewhere.

Now, there is one last note that will hopefully give you some peace of mind about doing readings. I have been asked the question, "What if I do a reading and it feels spot on, but the client later tells me that things did not work out the way their reading indicated? What went wrong?" Now, would you believe me if I said, "Nothing went wrong!"

Yes, once in a while you may be wrong with a message or an interpretation of information that is presented to you. You are human you know. We can get tired, feel sick, have a personal investment in a reading or be in a negative emotional state. Many other things can influence your reading as well.

However, if you feel clear and the information feels strong and resonates with you, trust it no matter what happens.

Remember that the reading and information that you impart to another is only good for the immediate timeframe. This is the energy for right now. Hmm, sounds funny? Once you impart information to your client, the outcome depends on the choices, decisions and actions of your client and you have no control over that. Here is an example of what I am speaking about.

During a reading for a client, the angels showed me a golden book around her head. This image is my symbol for authorship that yields a success. So I told the client what I was seeing and said that either she was thinking about writing a book or had already started one. Her response was, "Yes, I started a book several months ago, but hit writer's block and shelved the book." After I spoke to her about working with certain archangels for publishing, she left the reading feeling positive, uplifted, motivated and empowered.

Almost a year went by when this client phoned me to complain. She said that during her reading, I told her that the angels said her book was going to be a promising, successful book, but so far no publisher has accepted her book. She claimed that I was wrong and wanted to make sure that I knew it.

Sometimes because we are human, we can misinterpret information. When I am wrong, I admit it and politely say I am sorry. Some others in the metaphysical community have a strong belief that you never admit that you are wrong and never apologize. I believe in honesty. In this instance, the angels chimed in with information and I followed their lead.

They guided me to ask her how she felt about her reading. She responded, "Great, and I felt good about taking the book off the shelf and began writing again."

Then the angels wanted me to ask how she felt while preparing her manuscript for submission. After I inquired about her feelings, there was dead silence on the phone. I knew at that point that I hit on something. She said that she was motivated to complete her book, but remembered from her reading that the angels said the book would be successful and would yield much money. When an author becomes successful, it means traveling for book signing events and radio and television shows, which my client knew. She admitted that when she put her literary proposals together, she wished that her book would only be a little successful because she did not want to leave home for too long and do all of the traveling. Essentially, her very own deliberate intent and feelings limited her success and closed the doors.

Remember, the choices, decisions and actions that we take after a reading determine the final outcome. Yes, this is how it all works.

ADVANCED SELF-CARE PRACTICES

B eings in the angelic realm and spirit world vibrate at a much higher level than you do. Therefore, it is vital that you take good care of yourself energetically, practicing good spiritual hygiene at all times. This will help you to match your vibration to the angelic realm, forging a stronger and firmer connection while enhancing your ability to receive more messages with greater clarity and ease. Preparing for a reading means that you're clearing yourself energetically and creating sacred space within as well as all around you. Even when reading only for yourself, you will need to practice good spiritual hygiene.

Clearing Auras & Chakras

Just as taking a bath or shower cleanses our physical body, so does clearing the aura and chakras cleanse our individual energy field. Cleaning your aura and chakras on a daily basis is an excellent habit, and there are numerous ways to accomplish this.

Here is one clearing method that I like to use, in which I ask Archangel Michael to help me. "Archangel Michael, please be with me now. Come in very close to me and connect with my energy and essence. Michael, please clear me both inside and out, all of my chakras, para-chakras, conscious, subconscious and super-conscious mind, my Higher Self, soul and oversoul. Please clear my home and everything in my home, my vehicle and everything in my vehicle, energy grids, portals or vortexes of Light that are in my home and around me, Michael, in all directions of time, space and dimension. Clear out all excess energy, negativity, earthbound spirits, entities, lower vibrational energies and beings, psychic dirt, debris, slime, parasites and any being, energy or entity that is not from the Light or has been reprogrammed by the Light, or not 100% pure Light, all devices and implants, monitoring devices and negative elementals and any beacon, portal or vortex of Light that is used for darkness or the opposing forces. Michael, please shut those down now and take all of this back to the Source of Light from which it came! So it is! So it is done! Thank you!"

As a result of doing this clearing on a daily basis for over six years, there is a rainbow energy grid that runs through my home which I have captured on film. What nice validation from Michael that he is indeed present with me, creating sacred, holy and protective space!

There is another technique given to me by the angels, which I have named the "Metatron Cyclone." Again, it is a simple, easy yet powerful way to clear, clean and strengthen your auric field.

First, stand tall and firm (feet approximately 12 inches apart) and feel your feet on the ground. Next, call forth

Archangel Metatron and let your intention to clear your auric field be known.

Visualize a brilliant golden ring of Light beneath your feet, spinning all around you very rapidly–just like a cyclone. The ring of Light is infused with Metatron's energy and sacred geometric symbols like stars, diamonds, spheres and spirals, just to name a few. If you happen to get visuals on the shapes, trust. These symbols are embedded within this energy field and as it whirls all the chakras and para-chakras related to your feet are cleansed and cleared. When this feels complete, allow Metatron's cyclone to spiral around and up your body, clearing and cleaning each and every chakra and para-chakra that lies within your auric field.

As the Metatron cyclone whirls all around moving from the base of your feet all the way up to about two feet above your head, in your mind's eye see all of your charkas spin and glow with vibrant color and Light. All of your energy centers are now perfectly aligned and balanced, your entire auric field is pristine and the integrity field of its outer layers is at full strength.

As always, you may use this if you wish, change it, design your own or use any other technique that works for you.

The Violet Flame

The violet flame also referred to as the "Violet Fire," is a truly extraordinary sacred energy. To those who have developed their gift of clairvoyance, it is seen as violet in color, quite like the energy of the crown chakra. The violet flame possesses the unique ability to transmute negative energy into positive which makes it a very effective tool for clearing and healing.

Much like our skin absorbs cream or moisturizer, we sometimes absorb negative or heavy energy and the violet flame can purify us, as it transmutes energy that can make us feel depressed or heavy inside.

Here is a simple clearing technique utilizing the violet flame which can be done anywhere.

Stand up straight with your feet about 12 inches apart. Visualize the violet flame of transmutation in the pit or bottom of your stomach. Breathe in deeply, and then exhale out all negativity using the violet flame to push out the dense, heavy negative energy. Continue breathing in and exhaling out the old energy until you see or feel violet smoke coming out of your mouth.

Cord Cutting

Psychic etheric cords are created on a daily basis, a natural effect of our emotional responses. Energy cords can be positive such as those between you and your spouse, lover, children or your pets. Others can be negative and drain you of energy. These may be formed as a result of an argument with a friend, partner, boss, colleague, a family member or someone you know that does not like you and may even wish you harm. You may have heard the old saying, "If looks could kill, I would be dead." Well, when you experience a situation or person that gives you that feeling, it's likely they have sent some negative energy your way, unknowingly causing a negative, draining cord to be formed.

In truth, whenever we interact negatively with others, we create cords which contaminate and deplete their energy as well as our own.

Good spiritual hygiene is truly beneficial for everyone, and especially vital for those who conduct readings, angel sessions, healing and counseling. Fortunately, cord removal can be very simple.

Calling on Archangel Michael is one method. Say, "Archangel Michael with your blue flaming sword of love, please cut away and dissolve in all directions of time, space and dimension, all cords of attachment to me now and take them to the Light. Thank you, Michael!"

Another technique you can use is to call forth the violet flame of transmutation, directing it to dissolve away all cords or you may specify which cords you wish to remove.

You may create various affirmations and/or visualizations for cutting or removal of cords. The most important aspect of any method you select is your intent. One crucial note: You must honestly be willing to release these cords. This applies to all cording, and doubly so for any that you yourself may have brought into being.

Spirit Releasement

The aura or energy field can at times become weakened, even damaged. In this state, our vibratory rate may slow down, allowing lower vibrational beings or discarnate spirits and entities to attach themselves to us. There are a variety of ways in which this can happen:

- Addictions (alcohol and abuse of drugs or medications)

- Negative thought patterns

- Illness and disease

- Stress and anxiety

- Psychic attacks

- Poor spiritual hygiene

Note that if daily clearing, shielding and protection are practiced, spirit attachments may be avoided altogether, which is certainly preferable!

Even so, there may be times when you suspect or sense that the integrity of your energy field has been compromised.

Here are some indications which you may notice, or someone close to you may point out:

- Baffling physical ailments

- Feeling drained and even exhausted for no apparent reason

- Unexplained emotional instability

- Behavior that is out of character or personality changes

- Mood swings including depression and anxiety attacks

- Negative thoughts

- Nightmares

- Challenges with concentration and decision making

- Suicidal ideations

- Hearing voices that are negative or self degrading, giving you instructions to harm yourself or another

While nothing on the list is an absolute sign that you have an entity attachment, they are examples of how a spirit attachment can affect you.

As always, be sure to first seek medical advice from an appropriate health professional. If no cause can be pinpointed or no change is effected via prescribed treatment, it may be time to perform a spirit releasement. It will certainly do no harm and may prove instead be immensely beneficial! Physical and emotional health may immediately return to normal or medical interventions may suddenly begin to have the desired effects.

There are other ways attachments may come to your attention. Those who have honed their clairvoyant, clairsentient or other intuitive skills may see, feel or otherwise detect entities or heavier energy.

The crucial point to be noted in any situation regarding attachments is that fear is not only unnecessary, it is definitely counterproductive. These spirit or entity attachments must simply to be cleared and taken back to the Light.

Archangel Michael and his Band of Mercy are wonderful at removing discarnate spirits, entities and even alien or energy implants which can also raise emotional and physical havoc.

When called upon, Michael and his legion of angels can remove the spirit attachment and return the entity to the higher realms for healing and evolution.

Since we are speaking about Archangel Michael and clearing, it is time to address shielding and protection.

Shielding & Protection

Here are some traditional techniques which may be appropriate to your belief system, as well as some other new methods.

- Invoke Archangel Michael and your guardian angels to surround you with golden Light of protection.

- Ask Archangel Michael to assign four large warrior angels immediately, one to the North, South, East and West, to always guard and protect your home and everyone in your home including, all pets or living things, and everything in the home! Visualize two males and two females for balanced energy. You can also expand this out by asking that the warrior angels are placed around the perimeter of your property and even your vehicle. Be certain to say, "Thank you!"

- Sprinkle yourself and your space with Holy water.

- Wear, carry or use Rosary beads.

- Smudge by burning sage and/or frankincense.

- Wear a cross or place one over the door of the place where you conduct your readings.

- Use crystals such as Charoite, Black Tourmaline, Labradorite or Tibetan Tektites.

- Sacred geometry is another powerful tool for protection. Create within your mind's eye the star tetrahedron and ask your spiritual team what color would be the most appropriate color to use for shielding and protection. Then visualize the tetrahedron all around you.

- Use the Excalibur Sword of Protection as taken from Dr. Norma Milanovich from Merlin's Magic Workshop:

> Stand firm and tall facing EAST. See and feel the Sword of Excalibur in your hand and visualize emanating from the tip of the sword in all directions a bluish white light and energy. This will create a circle of protection all around you. Say: "In the name of God, I take in hand the sword of power, to fight all evil and aggression."

> "In the name of God, I build a protective shield around myself, my family, friends, and colleagues. All beings that are not in the Light cannot penetrate this shield, nor can they influence in any way the mental, emotional, spiritual or physical bodies of myself or anyone who is connected to me in any way."

Then turn in a clockwise fashion holding the sword out in front of you, visualizing the Light and energy streaming from the tip. Stop at the same place where you began. End with saying, "So Be It! So It Is!"

❧ Invoke the protection of the Divine Mother, Mother Mary. If you remember some of the older statues and pictures of Mary, she is often shown standing barefooted, with one foot on Planet Earth and the other crushing the serpent's head, which is the symbol for evil and the darker forces. Here is what I say when I invoke the protective energies of the Divine Mother:

"Dear Divine Mother, please be with me now. Come in very close to me and connect with my energy and essence as my energy and essence connects with yours.

Shower and cocoon me in your golden pink energy of love, Light, compassion and protection. Please guide, guard and protect all of my chakras, para-chakras, physical body and my health, all of my subtle bodies, conscious, subconscious and super-conscious mind, Higher Self, soul, oversoul, my home and all the things in my home, my vehicle and all the things in my vehicle.

Also, guide, guard and protect my spiritual practices and my spiritual businesses, all of my classes and teachings, all of my angel readings, intuitive counseling and healing sessions, all attunements I receive or give, my creative writing and publishing projects, all of my channeled angel messages, all those serving on the Divine Healing prayer team and all those requesting prayers and healing energy, my personal, professional and business reputation and all of my finances and anyone who is connected to me. Please guide, guard and protect them now. Thank you!"

Breaking Vows With Darkness

This section contains a method for breaking all vows with darkness as taken from Lynn Grabhorn's book, *Dear God, What's Happening to Us?* In her book, she talks about lifetimes that we have had dealing with the dark forces, which she calls "The Others." In this book she gives some very powerful tools to help us finally break our connection with the dark side, the contracts that we have made knowingly or unknowingly with "The Others."

I want to share the breaking of contracts and vows with you, thus giving you another effective protection tool.

Breaking of All Contracts and Vows With Darkness

The first and second steps are enormously simple, and require no physical discomfort. The third may cause you to feel a bit "out of it" for a couple of days, but truly, such feelings will be minor. In a physical place where you can find and feel a degree of peace and quiet in your surroundings and within yourself, gather a serenity about you, and a sureness of intent, and state either out loud or to yourself (best if done out loud). Note: To make the statements more personal and powerful, I have added within the brackets (*state your full name*).

1. Your Guide Team:

    I (*state your full name*), "From the Light of God that I AM, I hereby declare that my team of guides shall, as soon as any necessary transference can be made, be comprised only of 100% pure Light who have never been reprogrammed by entities of the dark."

2. Your Primary Guide:

    I (*state your full name*), "From the Light of God that I AM, I hereby declare the entity that is my Primary Guide shall be an entity of 100% pure Light that has never been reprogrammed by entities of the dark, with such change, if necessary, to be made as soon as possible."

3. Your Consciousness:

    a. I (*state your full name*), "From the Light of God that I am, I hereby declare that my consciousness mix should be converted, if necessary, to a mix of 100% pure Light of entities that have never been reprogrammed by those of the dark. I further declare that this conversion should take place as soon as possible, but preferably during evening hours as I sleep and as gently as possible in order that I might continue my normal daily routines."

b. I (*state your full name*), "From the Light of God that I am, I call forth that all things, whether animate or inanimate, within or around me, my home, yard, car, computer, phone /cell phone, TV and place of business, be immediately deactivated from use as "directional beacons" by those who are not of 100% pure Light. I further declare that when this has been accomplished, it shall be irrevocable and permanent."

c. I (*state your full name*), "From the Light of God that I am, I call forth that no energies, entities, or beings are to be allowed anywhere around me at any time that are not 100% pure Light. I further declare this to be irrevocable and permanent."

d. I (*state your full name*), "From the Light of God that I am, be it known that I hereby cancel all contracts and/or agreements I have made with ANY entity, in any time frame or in any reality that were not in my best interest or in the interest of the Light, or that were made with entities who were not of 100% pure Light. I further declare that the cancellation of all such contracts is to be irrevocable and permanent in all time frames and realities."

Remember, whenever you seek guidance, always demand that what comes through be only of 100% pure Light.

If you are using any divination tools, for example, pendulums, tarot cards, channeling, etc., declare the usual, "IN THE NAME OF THE LIGHT."

Karma Clearing

The term "karma" is a Sanskrit word that means the total sum of an individual's actions in this as well as past lifetimes. Each and every day, we create karma. Some karma is good and some not so good. It is my belief that Christ is the Master of forgiveness, so I work with Christ each day and do a daily karma clearing with him.

Here is how I do this:

"Dear Jesus, please be with me now. Come close to me and connect with my energy and essence.

Beloved Jesus, my brother in the Light of the Most High, I sincerely and humbly ask from one Master to another, that any mistakes I have made today or any pain or hurt that I have created, or any negative thoughts, feelings, words, actions, beliefs or judgments of myself or another, I ask that they be undone, pardoned, forgiven and healed in all directions of time, space and dimension right now. Thank you!"

In this new millennium within the new energies of Earth, the souls of Earth are at a quickening of remembrance. They are more rapidly experiencing and going through the awakening process.

As a steward of Earth and a Lightworker, destined to awaken fully, you are moving into leadership positions to assist the souls of Earth to awaken and evolve spiritually.

Here are some steps to self-empowerment that can guide you on your path.

- Make a firm commitment to your spirituality and to be of service.

- Choose your thoughts well for you are powerful manifestors.

- Make your choices carefully and practice discernment. Always ask, "Is this for my highest good and the good of all concerned?" Think more globally instead of locally.

- Discern the true intent behind each action and know whether it serves spirit or ego.

- Practice being the Observer and not the Participant.

- Schedule God time each day. Practice prayer (asking) and meditation (being and listening).

- Practice being in the PRESENT moment.

- Know that you are a Divine Radiant Being of Light that can never be qualified by human thought and feelings.

- Understand ENERGY and how it affects you.

- Work daily on balancing your ENERGY for this will allow you to remain centered and peaceful at all times, even in the midst of total chaos. Centeredness puts you on the path to spiritual mastery.

- Practice compassionate detachment so that outside dramas cannot influence, manipulate or control you.

- Shift your perception and see Miracles everywhere you look!

- Practice the gift of Gratitude by saying "Thank you" for everything, especially your challenges.

- Resolve all your conflicts in the higher realms. Allow the Masters of Light along with the angels and other celestial beings to work on your behalf.

- Align your will with the Divine will for there is perfection in this and no duality.

- Begin to work with the Ascended Masters and your angels. Partner with the Divine and these Beings of Light. Ascended Masters are Illuminated Beings of Light who work for God and assist and serve humanity in the higher realms. They are powerful teachers, healers and leaders of the world whose sole purpose is to assist those who are serious about their spiritual mastery and the ascension path.

Remember that the soul is the gateway to higher consciousness and ascension. According to Ascended Master Kuthumi as channeled by Dr. Norma Milanovich, "Once the soul has removed all of its energy blockages, it is placed in a position to choose higher states of existence. This is a time when discernment and focus become critical for the soul's advancement. When the blockages are removed, energy begins to flow more freely. In this state, many choices may come to the individual. It is advisable to use the intuitive process to determine that which is of the highest interest for the individual in making the choices for one's path."

A Guidebook For Advanced Angel Readings

MORALS & ETHICS
OF ANGEL READINGS FOR OTHERS

Reading Ethics

When conducting angel sessions and readings, there is a Code of Ethics, which requires your careful consideration.

Best known as the Golden Rule, this principle should always come first and foremost in all aspects of your work and life: Do no harm, and treat others as you would want to be treated yourself.

Be respectful of your gifts and of others. Always get permission from your client before you do a reading, and never impose yourself on another. It is essential to respect every individual's free will. Violation of free will also constitutes "Harm."

If you ever receive a warning message for your client, please deliver it with compassion. Ask Archangel Michael to help you deliver the message of warning with Love.

Client confidentiality is very important. Keep your angel readings private and confidential unless you have permission from your client to share their information. If you ever feel guided to share some aspect of a reading for any reason, be certain to keep client identifiers completely and absolutely private. Identifiers are anything that can link your client's name and identity to the reading.

While doing readings, you may hear anything and everything, including affairs, addictions, sexual abuse, trauma, criminal activity or a multitude of other disconcerting activities. Be impartial and do not judge anyone. However, any suspected child abuse must be reported by law! Furthermore, if someone talks about murdering another person or themselves, you must report it. Impartiality applies in innumerable other ways as well and you should always be prepared for the unexpected. One of my appointments was with a male who showed up dressed as a woman, and it would have been inappropriate to make fun or judge.

If the angels reveal sensitive information during a reading, it is not your place to admonish anyone or prescribe personal advice.

However, if during the reading you want to give your own feedback, please acknowledge this to your client, indicating that what you are about to say is coming from you! Also, while it can be useful to share a brief personal story to help clarify a point, try not to talk about yourself during your reading session. This is your client's time.

Referring Your Client

In your angel reading practice, you may at times need to refer clients elsewhere. If so, this simply may mean that you are not the right reader for the client at this time or the client is not ready for this type of reading.

Relax, trust, respect and honor yourself and your client, and then refer them to another practitioner. Please do not take it personally!

Here are some instances of when you may want to refer a client to another reader or even to a different type of professional.

If your reading is not flowing or you are not getting anything, please be honest with your client and tell them the truth. At this point, graciously refund their money and refer them to another reader. Honesty is the best policy! Dishonesty is a grave disservice not only to the client, but to yourself as well, as this lowers your vibration, stifles your angelic connection and erodes your spiritual growth.

Some other examples include:

- When you see/sense your client's angels pull away

- Your client makes you angry

- When your stomach tightens and something does not feel right

- If you are attracted to your client

- If the reading is beyond your scope of experience, like someone who is suicidal or needing a mental health professional

It is not always easy to recognize depression, however some of the signs include: flat voice tone, rigid body, no energy, lifeless eyes, complaints of depression, lack of focus and concentration, sadness and crying. Should you suspect or feel concerned that a client might be suicidal, ask the person if they have a plan. If they do, refer them to a mental health professional and encourage your client to contact one immediately.

Have your own referral list ready. When a mental health professional (psychologist or psychotherapist) seems necessary because of a client's depression or suicidal feelings, you can gently say to this person, "It's not my area of expertise and here is someone who can help."

When beginning your angel practice, put out to the universe the type of clients you want to work with. Naturally, you will want to work with those who will receive blessings from you and those who will bring you blessings, in every way. Keep in mind that you don't have to accept every client. Refer out to another practitioner if you need to or are led to. If in doubt, refer out.

Setting Boundaries

It is important, if not vital to set boundaries with clients. Remember to take care of yourself by starting and ending sessions on time.

If your client is clearly attracted to you or you to them, it would be wise to take them off your client list.

As with most other professions, it is best to keep friendships and your professional life separate. Honor and keep your boundaries and learn to set limits. Always keep the messages focused on the angels. Avoid discussing yourself or your experiences unless you are guided to. Remember to ask for help. Trust what you see, feel, think or hear and be willing to share the message with love.

The most important thing is to TRUST your guidance.

BUILDING YOUR ANGEL READING PRACTICE

Here are some basic helpful guidelines and tips that can assist you in building your spiritual practice.

1. First, come out of the closet about your spiritual work.

2. Mentally roll out the red carpet for clients and students, and send out positive energy.

3. Partner with God, Archangel Michael, Archangel Gabriel and your guardian angels to help you to build your practice. Develop and form a co-creative business partnership. Discuss ideas and decisions with your Heavenly business team.

4. When applying for a teaching or reading position, include a copy of your certificate(s) in your submission packet. This presents you as a professional for those who wish to see credentials.

5. Network with other Lightworkers and share referrals, for there is enough work for everyone.

6. Conduct workshops at metaphysical bookstores. If you are nervous and scared, ask Archangel Michael for courage.

7. Write a small article for a new age or metaphysical magazine. You can try a new thought church such as the Unitarian or Spiritualist Church.

8. Offer free lectures at libraries, specialty groups or clubs such as cancer support groups, the Rotary Club or other organizations.

9. Place your business cards and brochures out in the community and carry them with you, for you never know when you are going to have an angel appointment. If you don't put your cards and brochures out, then no one will know you are in business or will call you.

10. You can do angel reading parties, psychic fairs and readings at metaphysical bookstores.

12. Don't give out your home address to just anyone. If you are doing readings in your home, alert someone (friend, neighbor and/or spouse) that you are having a client(s) over. Just be smart and use common sense!

13. Offer phone and internet readings. You can set up credit card payment options using "Pay Pal" or "Pro Pay." You can either set up your own website or you can become a professional Internet reader through other internet sites that offer psychic readings.

14. Because many states are now instituting state laws about doing spiritual healing, it would be important

to consider becoming an ordained minister. You can become an ordained Interfaith Minister through the Universal Life Church in CA. This protects you as a hands-on healer as well as allowing you access to hospitals and churches. You can apply for your certification at http://ulc.org.

15. Do good work for it is your very best advertiser and word of mouth travels fast. If you do choose to advertise, carefully research to find the most inexpensive and effective way to advertise in your area.

16. Create a website for your services.

17. Avoid problems with clients owing you payment by working with Archangel Gabriel. If someone owes you for services already delivered and your client is tardy with payment, please just say, "Archangel Gabriel, please be with me now. Archangel Gabriel, I completed a reading for Mark three weeks ago, so would you please prompt him to pay me in full and oversee the quick, efficient and safe delivery of those monies to me now, and thank you."

18. Practice integrity, honesty and always keep your word.

19. Develop certification programs.

20. Do What You Love and Love What You Do!

As a Lightworker, your most profound responsibility is to teach love through your choices and actions. Choose love, peace and healing as your path for growth and when you do, your business will grow faster.

Appendix

BOOK RESOURCES

Astell, Christine. *Discovering Angels*. London, England: Duncan Baird Publishers, 2005.

Bunson, Matthew. *Angels A to Z*. New York, NY: Three Rivers Press, 1996.

Choquette Ph.D., Sonia. *The Psychic Pathway*. New York, NY: Three Rivers Press, 1994.

Farmer Ph.D., Steven D. *Animal Spirit Guides*. Carlsbad, CA: Hay House, Inc., 2006.

Foley, Elizabeth J. *Angel Readings for Beginners*. Nashua, NH: Angel Street Publishing, LLC., 2009.

Foley, Elizabeth J. *Awakening the Lightworker Within: A Personal Journey of Answering the Sacred Call*. Nashua, NH: Angel Street Publishing, LLC., 2008.

Guiley, Rosemary Ellen. *Ask the Angels*. Charlottesville, VA: Hampton Roads Publishing Company, 2008.

Guiley, Rosemary Ellen. *The Encyclopedia of Angels*. New York, NY: Checkmark Books, 2004.

Milanovich, Norma Dr. *The Light Shall Set You Free*. Scottsdale, AZ: Athena Publishing, 1996.

O'Brien, Stephen. *The Power of Your Spirit: Develop Your Natural Psychic Abilities*. Swansea, United Kingdom: Voices, 2003.

Pielmeier, Heidemarie, Schirner, Marcus. *Illustrated Tarot Spreads: 78 New Layouts for Personal Discovery.* New York, NY: Sterling Publishing Company, 1995.

Prophet, Elizabeth Clare. *Violet Flame.* Corwin Springs, MO: Summit University Press, 2003.

Prophet, Mark, Prophet, Elizabeth Clare. *The Masters and their Retreats.* Corwin Springs, MO: Summit University Press, 1997.

Raven, Hazel. *The Angel Bible.* New York, NY: Sterling Publishing Company, Inc, 2006.

Roman, Sanaya, Packer, Duane. *Opening to Channel: How to Connect with Your Guide.* Tiburon, CA: H J Kramer, Inc, 1987.

Virtue, Doreen. *Divine Guidance.* Los Angeles, CA: Renaissance Books, 1998.

Virtue, Doreen. *Earth Angels.* Carlsbad, CA: Hay House, Inc., 2002.

Virtue, Doreen. *The Lightworker's Way.* Carlsbad, CA: Hay House, Inc., 1997.

Wauters, Ambika. *The Book of Chakras.* Hauppauge, NY: Barron's Educational Series, 2002.

ACKNOWLEDGEMENTS

To my amazing angelic support team, Archangel Michael, Archangel Gabriel, my guardian angels, the Ascended Masters and the many other spiritual beings that guide and support me in all ways.

I am deeply grateful to a very special friend, colleague and soul sister, Allison. She gave me the perseverance to keep moving ahead and assisted with the writing of this book.

Many writing assistants came to my aid, so a special thank you to Cathy Corcoran and Robin Wrighton who bring magic to my creative projects.

Most of all, thank you to the many students and angel clients throughout the years. You have been wonderful teachers for me and I am truly blessed by your presence in my life.

ABOUT THE AUTHOR

Elizabeth J. Foley, EdM, MPH is an international Angelologist, teacher, healer, radio talk show host and author. She holds Master degrees in Counseling and Guidance and in Public Health. She is a doctoral candidate in Metaphysics at the American Institute of Holistic Theology and has appeared on various radio and television shows including the Liz Walker Show-WBZ 4 Boston. Elizabeth conducts private angel sessions and facilitates unique spiritual workshops on angels, psychic development and Soul Therapy throughout the country. She makes her home in Nashua, NH. For more information, please visit www.divinehealing.us.

ANGEL HEALING PRACTITIONER CERTIFICATION PROGRAM

The Angel Healing Practitioner© certification course encourages you to awaken your intuition, read energy, conduct angel readings confidently and to learn and practice angel healing techniques. You will also discover the ways in which the angelic realm communicates with you and learn to receive messages, information and Divine guidance and healing from the angels.

The main objective of the course is to:

♥ Teach you how to give accurate and healing angel readings, explore various card spreads and how to interpret the meaning.

♥ Help you discover your natural Divine communication style and how to combine clairvoyance, clairaudience, clairsentience and claircognizance with your card readings to gain deeper insight and understanding of your angels' messages.

♥ Learn about the angelic realm including information about guardian angels, archangels, Ascended Masters, fairies and deceased loved ones.

♥ Teach you how to prepare yourself and your cards for conducting an angel reading.

♥ Practice automatic writing with the angels for receiving messages and information.

♥ Learn and practice angel healing techniques for self and others.

♥ Become familiar with the practical and ethical considerations involved in becoming an Angel Healing Practitioner©.

♥ Learn techniques to build your practice.

For more information and dates, please contact Elizabeth J. Foley at Divine Healing, P.O. Box 7124, Nashua, NH 03060 or visit www.divinehealing.us.

SOUL THERAPY PRACTITIONER CERTIFICATION PROGRAM

Each of us has a unique Divine soul and soul mission and the Soul Therapy Practitioner© (STP) Program is dedicated to an in-depth discovery, healing and clearing of the different aspects of your mental, emotional, physical and spiritual bodies. The goal of the STP program is to help you discover and align your inner spiritual life with your outer life and to empower yourself and others. In this powerful certification course, not only will you embark on your own inner sacred quest, but you also will learn how to assist others on their spiritual journey and discovery. This program is limited to eight people only and attendance is required for all four weekends.

The Soul Therapy Practitioner© program is a four weekend self-guided program that includes:

♥   What is the Soul and Understanding the Energy of Your Soul

♥   Listening and Connecting to Your Soul

♥   Understanding and Opening the Seven Seals (spiritual issues and the chakras)

♥   The Seven Rays and How They Guide Your Soul

♥   Development of the Soul (discovering your soul age, level and role)

♥   Basics of Spiritual Psychology (exploring the twelve life lessons & creating a spiritual psychological profile)

♥   Awakening and Clearing the Physical, Mental, Emotional and Spiritual Body

♥   Tools for Emotional and Spiritual Healing

♥   Tests of Initiation of the Soul

♥   Steps to Attain Mastery and Manifest Your Mission

For more information and dates, please contact Elizabeth J. Foley at Divine Healing, P.O. Box 7124, Nashua, NH 03060 or visit www.divinehealing.us.

ANGEL STREET PUBLISHING, LLC

OTHER TITLES BY THIS AUTHOR

BOOKS

Awakening the Lightworker Within:
A Personal Journey of Answering the Sacred Call

Angel Readings for Beginners

CARD DECKS

Nature Spirits Oracle Cards

CDs

Meditations for Healing and Spiritual Transformation
with Elizabeth Foley